"In a day of heightened awareness ([...] important that Christians know how t [...] Muslim for the hope that is in us. Sinc [...] of the crucifixion, burial, and resurrection of Jesus, the evidence for these events constitutes justification for thinking that Christianity rather than Islam gives us the truth about Jesus and the God he revealed. In this book Licona not only marshals that evidence but also refutes the typical objections brought by Muslim apologists against it."

William Lane Craig, research professor of philosophy,
Talbot School of Theology

"The Islam/Christian debate all comes down to whether Jesus rose from the dead shortly after his crucifixion. If he did not, then Christianity is a sham. In his book, *Paul Meets Muhammad*, Michael Licona entertains and educates the reader with an ingeniously crafted debate that is fair to both sides. If you are a Christian looking for a resource on how to share your faith with your Muslim friend, look no further."

D. James Kennedy, senior minister, Coral Ridge Presbyterian Church,
Fort Lauderdale, Florida; chancellor, Knox Theological Seminary

"Reconstructing debates between the greats of the past is a clever device occasionally attempted in the media—printed or aired—but never with such success as in *Paul Meets Muhammad*. St. Paul debating Muhammad? Forget the time warp and simply enjoy the interchange! Since Michael Licona is fast becoming one of Christianity's most eloquent apologists for the resurrection, you will assume a strong, pro-Christian bias in this book (St. Paul will have all the good lines and Muhammad the bad) but you will be wrong! Licona brilliantly presents also the Muslim arguments at the heart of the Christian-Muslim dialogue, claims that Jesus never died and so could not have been resurrected. Since the Muslim challenge to the church is becoming more acute each passing day, it is well for Christians to arm themselves with the arsenal of arguments presented in these pages."

Paul L. Maier, professor of history, Western Michigan University

"This brilliant idea for reconstructing a dialogue between Paul and Mohammad plainly indicates Mike Licona's mastery of the subject matter of Jesus's resurrection. Islam postulates an alternate theory that is supernatural in nature. This book successfully critiques this approach and needs to be read by any Christian desiring to have constructive dialogue with Muslims. Since Mike's presentation of the Muslim view is actually stronger than I have heard presented by Muslim scholars, Muslims should enjoy reading it, too!"

Gary Habermas, distinguished research professor, Liberty University

"Paul Meets Muhammad is appropriately titled. In this book Michael Licona makes plain the differences that exist between Christianity and Islam concerning the central truth of the Christian faith: the historical, bodily resurrection of Jesus, the Son of God. The debate format between the apostle Paul and the prophet Muhammad will draw one quickly into the discussion. Licona's treatment of the issue, fair and balanced, draws on primary sources which allows each side to speak for themselves. The importance of historically credible evidence, careful reasoning, and logical consistency are clearly demonstrated. Read this book and learn. Read this book and be challenged. Read this book and see evidence mount for the empty tomb and the supernatural resurrection of Jesus Christ."

Donald L. Akin, president, Southeastern Baptist Theological Seminary

"An engaging and delightful debate between St. Paul and Muhammad! Mike Licona does a splendid job of laying out the key differences between Christianity and Islam, which center on the historicity and theological significance of Jesus's death and resurrection."

Paul Copan, Pledger Family Chair of Philosophy and Ethics, Palm Beach Atlantic University

"Michael Licona's *Paul Meets Muhammad* highlights the key points of disagreement between Christian and Islamic faith in a way that is easy to understand and fun to read. The imaginary debate between the Paul the apostle and Muhammad the prophet is fair and respectful and will help Muslims and Christians alike to understand better the importance and centrality of the resurrection of Jesus. Although advanced students of religion will find this book useful and stimulating, it will prove especially helpful to non-experts. I highly recommend it."

Craig A. Evans, Payzant Distinguished Professor, Acadia Divinity College, Nova Scotia, Canada

"In his new book *Paul Meets Muhammad*, Michael R. Licona has, in one fell swoop, found the most unique manner of approaching Islamic evangelism that I have seen in quite some time. Licona is intelligent, on target, strong in conviction, and yet at the same time compassion and sensitivity flow through this work. I cannot give this work a higher endorsement. Buy it, use it. This book can change lives."

Ergun Mehmet Caner, dean, Liberty Theological Seminary

"In this book one finds creativity mixed with solid information, resulting in a very interesting reading experience. Its biggest contribution is its honest attempt to introduce readers to the Christian-Islam debate, one that will only become more and more important in our global village."

Jan van der Watt, professor of New Testament studies, University of Pretoria

Paul Meets Muhammad

A Christian-Muslim Debate on the Resurrection

Michael R. Licona

BakerBooks

Grand Rapids, Michigan

© 2006 by Michael R. Licona

Published by Baker Books
a division of Baker Publishing Group
P.O. Box 6287, Grand Rapids, MI 49516-6287
www.bakerbooks.com

Printed in the United States of America

Library of Congress Cataloging-in-Publication Data
Licona, Mike, 1961–
   Paul meets Muhammad : a Christian-Muslim debate on the
   Resurrection / Michael R. Licona.
      p.   cm.
   Includes bibliographical references. (p.   )
   ISBN 0-8010-6602-6 (pbk.)
      1. Jesus Christ—Resurrection. 2. Paul, the Apostle, Saint.
   3. Muhammad, Prophet, d. 632. 4. Christianity and other reli-
   gions—Islam. 5. Islam—Relations—Christianity. I. Title.
   BT482.L53 2006
   232′.5—dc22   2005027486

Unless otherwise indicated, Scripture quotations are the author's own translation from the original Greek.

Scripture marked NASB is taken from the New American Standard Bible®, Copyright © 1960, 1962, 1963, 1968, 1971, 1972, 1973, 1975, 1977, 1995 by The Lockman Foundation. Used by permission.

Scripture marked NLT is taken from the Holy Bible, New Living Translation, copyright © 1996. Used by permission of Tyndale House Publishers, Inc., Wheaton, Illinois 60189. All rights reserved.

Scripture marked NRSV is taken from the New Revised Standard Version of the Bible, copyright 1989, Division of Christian Education of the National Council of the Churches of Christ in the United States of America. Used by permission. All rights reserved.

Quotations from the Qur'an cited in this book are from The Meaning of The Holy Qur'an, New Edition with Revised Translation, Commentary and Newly Compiled Comprehensive Index, 10th edition, trans. Abdullah Yusuf Ali (Beltsville, MD: Amana, 1999). All rights reserved. Used with permission.

To my mom and dad. Thank you for enduring my teens, encouraging and assisting me, and being there for me even afterward. I love you lots!

Contents

Foreword

I sat horrified as I watched the unthinkable: the World Trade Center buildings in New York City were collapsing after Muslim terrorists slammed two hijacked commercial jetliners into them. As the buildings were crumbling into rubble, America's awareness of Islam began soaring to unprecedented heights.

Several years have passed since that tragic September 11th of 2001, but Islam continues to be in the news daily. Few of the articles, though, deal with the issue that I'm particularly interested in: Is the world's second largest faith the true religion that it claims to be?

Some people think it's impossible to make a judgment about the truth of religious assertions. However, I'm convinced that the same logic that has enabled humankind to make remarkable advances in science also permits us to adjudicate matters of faith.

For instance, if two statements contradict each other, it's safe to say that they both cannot be true. Both could be false or either one could be true, but they both cannot be true at the same time and in the same way. Consider the following statements:

- The Boston Red Sox were the 2004 World Series Baseball Champions.
- The Chicago Cubs were the 2004 World Series Baseball Champions.

Although these are both truth claims, obviously both of the statements cannot be true. There is the possibility that that one or the other could be true. And if we were to substitute "New York Yankees" for the "Boston Red Sox"—as many in New York would gladly do—then we could see that both statements were false, since neither the Yankees nor the Cubs were the 2004 World Series Champions.

Now let's consider the following two truth claims:

- Christianity is the one true religion.
- Islam is the one true religion.

The New Testament of the Bible and Islam's holy book, the Qur'an, make these claims. Both cannot be true. Either both are false (that is, God does not exist or another religion, such as Hinduism, is true) or one or the other is true.

We could go on the Internet and examine archived articles to discover the truth about who actually won the 2004 World Series. Finding the answer to the conflicting truth claims of Christianity and Islam, however, is much more difficult. We have to dig for the facts and consider them carefully. Even though the topic is supremely important, most people lack both the time and the training to sort through the issues for themselves.

That's why I'm so excited about this book. The author, Mike Licona, is a Christian scholar who's an expert on the resurrection of Jesus, which is the historical linchpin of Christianity. He has debated one of Islam's leading experts on two occasions and is highly qualified to write on this topic.

Mike has been a guest twice on my national television program Faith Under Fire, once sparring with a liberal Christian scholar and the other time debating a Muslim on the deity of Jesus. One thing's for sure: Mike doesn't give pat answers or merely echo stock Christian arguments. Instead, he has been willing to wrestle with tough questions and emerge with fresh insights as a result.

Whether you're a Christian, a Muslim, or someone else who's seeking to discover truth, I believe you're going to find this book to be a fascinating and challenging experience. So go ahead—read it, give it to your Muslim friend, and let the dialogue begin!

Lee Strobel
author, *The Case for Christ*

Acknowledgments

I would like to thank the following for reading earlier drafts of this book and for their very helpful criticisms and suggestions. Their contributions were invaluable. In alphabetical order: Kathy Laser, Debbie Licona, Jacki Payne, Amy Ponce, Nabeel Qureshi, David Wood, Marie Wood. I am especially grateful to Nabeel, who, being a Muslim friend when he read an early manuscript of this book, provided comments where he believed my understanding of Islam needed correction. In the course of time prior to the release of this book, however, Nabeel's own journey led him to become a Christian. Amy was also especially helpful in providing ideas for chapter 1.

Introduction

Although Christianity remains the world's largest religion, Islam is the fastest-growing religion. Understandably, therefore, the issue of truth often comes up in discussions between Muslims and Christians. Apologists from both religions provide evidence for the truth of their religions, ranging from the miracles and claims of Jesus to scientific evidence supporting the Qur'an's divine origin. Much debate continues in these areas.

Since Jesus's resurrection is the foundation of the Christian faith and is an event denied by Islam's holy Scripture called the Qur'an, both Muslims and Christians can agree upon two things: (1) *If Jesus did not rise from the dead, Christianity is false*, and (2) *if Jesus was resurrected, Christianity is true and Islam is false*. The resurrection of Jesus, therefore, is a good topic for discussion among Muslims and Christians. Did it occur? Is the evidence strong enough that a rational person would be justified in believing that it occurred merely based on the evidence?

The objective of this book is to assist Muslims and Christians in understanding the discussion and in making an informed assessment of the evidence, the arguments, and the conclusions on the resurrection of Jesus that each faith promotes. I admit from the outset that I am a Christian and therefore bring to this book my personal conviction that strong historical evidence exists for the bodily resurrection of Jesus. I have worked hard to minimize the effect that conviction might have on this volume by stating the most common and relevant Islamic objections as forcefully as I could, sometimes even attempting to strengthen their current form. I also asked one of my Muslim friends (I have several) to read the manuscript and provide suggestions, most of which I have incorporated into the text. I realize that I have still fallen short and ask especially for the forgiveness and patience of the Muslim reader.

Many readers may ask why this is a debate between Muhammad and Paul rather than Muhammad and Jesus. It was a difficult choice. Muslims view Jesus and Muhammad as great prophets and Paul as a false apostle. Christians view Jesus as divine, Paul as one of the greatest apostles, and Muhammad as a false prophet. Thus they can reach no agreement on who is a peer. I have two reasons for casting this debate as I have. First, the claims of both Muhammad and Paul to have experienced supernatural revelation which led to their life of proselytizing others to their religious views makes them natural dialogue partners. Second, while both Christians and Muslims agree that Jesus was a great person who brought a message and authority from God, Muslims reject the authority of Paul, while Christians reject the authority of Muhammad. Thus these would seem again to be a natural match.

The views expressed by Paul and Muhammad herein represent both specific claims and arguments each man made while alive and statements of modern religious scholarship on both sides. Naturally, Paul and Muhammad never got to discuss these topics with each other, and thus I've crafted a fictional setting for this debate to pose the ultimate "what if?"

My hope is that God will use this small contribution as a tool for creating productive and friendly dialogue on this issue between Muslims and Christians. Unless otherwise noted, all quotations from the New Testament are my own translation from the original Greek.

Michael Licona
August 2005

1

Into the Future

Many exuberant conversations take place simultaneously as nearly three hundred members of the press fill the Tang Center's Wong Auditorium on the campus of MIT. Three people talk with one another on the stage. The third, who is more sharply dressed than the others, breaks away from the other two and approaches the microphone. "Good morning, everyone. Thanks for coming. I'm Robert Gordon, president of MIT. Prior to my arrival at MIT, two esteemed scientists were commissioned to come up with a scientific process for making educated guesses as to how those in the past who were known for their wisdom would have responded to contemporary crises. The two scientists selected were Dr. Ahmad Bahkr and Dr. Rebecca Sweeney. After fifteen years of persistent effort, the project known as Project Resurrection has achieved a level of success that could only have been dreamed of a few years ago. I've brought Dr. Ahmad Bahkr to explain everything to you. Dr. Bahkr is the director of Project Resurrection."

A man dressed in a blue suit approaches the podium. He is in his midfifties and of Middle Eastern descent and speaks very clearly with an accent that is hardly detectable. "Good morning. For the past fifteen years, Dr. Sweeney and I have been working on a project named Resurrection. This project is designed to simulate how a person of a different era known for his wisdom might yield fresh insights for dealing with present world conditions such as hunger, disease, and volatile political differences. Project Resurrection works by entering into a computer database all of the known writings of a person, credible reports about him or her from outside sources, and additional data on that person from modern experts. Using quasi-artificial intelligence, the computer is able to *think* as that particular person would by identifying the person's specific thought patterns, personality traits, and worldview. As a result, the computer can suggest how that person might have responded to a contemporary crisis, such as AIDS or terrorism, or even provide military strategy. We have been very pleased with what we've been able to accomplish and have arranged a public demonstration. I will now take your questions."

At this point it becomes loud as many reporters begin asking questions. Dr. Bahkr points to a woman in the front row, who stands and says, "Peggy Jasper of CNN. Would you tell us something about the accuracy of Project Resurrection?"

"We've been able to achieve a high level of accuracy," Bahkr replies. "About a year ago, we conducted initial testing. We entered the writings and speeches of the two final candidates from the most recent presidential election and played out a debate between them. Accuracy was measured by comparing the simulated debate with the historical one. Adjustments were made to the artificial intelligence component. The simulated debate was reenacted and a number of similar experiments were performed as well in order to test and gain further precision. We were amazed to observe an increase in accuracy from approximately 65 to 88 percent over a period of ten months.

"Then we put Project Resurrection through a second stage of tests in which we entered the writings of the famous philosophers atheist Bertrand Russell and Christian Frederick Copleston and simulated a debate between them on the existence of God. The results corresponded to their actual 1948 debate with staggering accuracy. Presently Project Resurrection is operating with an approximate accuracy of 95 percent and an error margin of plus or minus 3 percent. This accuracy is contingent upon entering a minimum of only two megabytes of information about the historical person being considered. I would now like to ask my colleague Dr. Sweeney to tell you about another amazing feature of this project."

A woman in her early fifties, with slightly graying hair curling under just short of her shoulders, approaches the podium. She clears her throat quietly and begins to speak. "Good morning. Three months ago, Dr. Bahkr and I incorporated Virtua-Personi 6.0 hologram technology with voice recognition capabilities into Project Resurrection. This enabled us to have both a visual and a virtual reality interactive experience. We can now watch the selected person lecture, carry on a conversation, debate, ask questions, and receive advice. We conducted our first test using holograms one month ago. I had a discussion with Socrates and was absolutely astonished by how real it seemed. I could hardly tell the difference from a real person. I went home that night feeling as though I had been in the presence of an icon. I couldn't sleep at all that evening."

At this moment a reporter blurts out, "What are your plans for using Project Resurrection?"

Dr. Sweeney replies, "The United States government has been aware of our research and has demanded that it be allowed to purchase the fully completed project for military purposes. A separate version containing a software block prohibiting military use will be made available for sale to corporations within a year."

Another reporter calmly asks, "What will the price tag be?"

Dr. Sweeney appears unprepared to answer the question and turns around to look at Bahkr and Gordon. The university president is very aware of the proposed sales price and steps up to the podium. He says, "That will depend on the corporate package purchased. For example, a robust package that includes hologram technology will have a much higher price tag than a package that doesn't include it. A complete package will probably be in the range of five hundred million dollars."

A hum of conversation starts throughout the auditorium at this revelation. Gordon sits down, and Sweeney steps back to the podium and points to her left, "The gentleman over there."

"When can we see a demonstration of the corporate product?"

"As a promotion, we will stage a public exhibition in three months involving a debate between two famous persons from antiquity."

"Have you chosen which two persons you will use?"

"Yes. My colleague Dr. Jeffrey Bowers from the Department of Philosophy here at MIT can tell you more."

Dr. Sweeney steps away from the podium as a man in his midfifties, with a medium build and gray hair, walks from where he had been standing next to the wall on the side of the auditorium to Sweeney's right. He steps up onto the stage and comes up to the podium. He appears to be very comfortable in front of a large audience. "The apostle Paul and the prophet Muhammad have been chosen to be our debaters," Dr. Bowers says. "We have an abundance of ancient writings by or about these figures, so they will be very suitable as debate opponents. The topic will be the foundational event of Christianity: the resurrection of Jesus."

He motions to a journalist in the front row, who stands and asks, "Aren't you afraid that such a debate could create serious religious tensions between Christian and Muslim communities?"

Bowers does not hesitate. "We thought about that, and the consensus among us is that since this is a fictional debate and the topic does not concern whether Christianity or Islam is true or false, tensions should be kept to a minimum. Indeed, we're hoping that such a debate will provide followers of both religions with a greater understanding of where the other is coming from. However, just to be on the safe side, adequate security will be provided for the debate. Yes, sir. Over there. You have a question?"

"Where and when will this debate take place?"

"We are in the process of making arrangements with TCN Field in Birmingham, Alabama, since it has a retractable roof. Then if the weather turns sour on us, we'll be okay. We don't have a firm date at this time. But if all goes well, we should have a debate in about three months, which will be late June."

At this point Robert Gordon approaches the podium and places his hand on Bowers's back, signaling that he wants to wrap things up. Bowers moves to the side and Gordon takes the lead spot at the podium. "Thank you, Dr. Bowers. Ladies and gentlemen, this is a noble project, and I speak on behalf of everyone here at MIT in saying that we are excited about seeing this technological leap. We are interested in doing our best to contribute to solving world crises. We are interested in helping our country, and therefore the world, become a safer place for us to live. Thank you for coming, ladies and gentlemen. We'll look forward to seeing you in Birmingham."

The night of the debate has come. The stadium is packed with corporate leaders from around the world. The event will be televised, broadcast over the Internet, heard by radio, and a transcript will be made available. All the major television networks are present, and the entire world is tuning in with great interest. In order to get the most accurate feel for the "reality" factor, Dr. Bahkr and Dr. Sweeney have taken seats among the crowd in the stadium. They are surrounded by undercover guards strategically positioned in their section. The stadium holds a capacity crowd of sixty thousand, and the air is peppered with various perfumes and colognes and the aromas normally sensed at professional American sporting events—beverages, hot dogs (all beef, of course!), hamburgers, mustard, popcorn, and cotton candy. Numerous languages can be heard in the plethora of simultaneous conversations. Not surprisingly, Arabic and English are dominant.

A strong police presence is visible in the crowd in order to thwart any show of aggression toward those of different beliefs. Long lines leading to massive security checks mark every entrance to the stadium. About ninety minutes of sunlight remain. The stadium lights are on in preparation for the approaching sunset and are brighter than the evening sky, which is clear and cloudless. The American flag can be seen flapping in the gentle breeze on this beautiful evening. Anticipation is felt by every faithful follower, wondering how well Paul and Muhammad will be represented and who will win the debate.

Because English is the most universal language, it will be the language of choice for the evening's speakers. Various concessionaires walk around offering beverages, food, and battery-powered wireless headsets that will provide translation services. No music is played. The scoreboard displays a message: "Please respect one another. Aggressors will be removed immediately from the premises." Every twenty seconds the scoreboard displays the same message in a different language.

Dr. Sweeney looks at her watch, then looks at Dr. Bahkr, who glances at his. "It's time," he says. Just then a hush quickly falls on the crowd as three black Mercedes-Benz sedans drive onto the field and up to the stage which has been set up in the center. When the cars come to a halt, ten men dressed in suits jump out of the first and third cars. Five of them form a scattered line up to the stage, and two take their positions at the rear corners of the stage. The other three approach the middle car. One opens the front passenger's side door while the other two open the rear doors on each side. Simultaneously, three men emerge. The man from the front is the moderator for the debate, Dr. Jeffrey Bowers.

Out of the backseat on the same side of the car steps a man of average height. He wears a turban on his head, a beard that is nearly twelve inches long, and a long gown that is fairly plain in style and not very colorful. It is Muhammad. Out of the other side of the car emerges Paul, also of average height and with a beard that is cut fairly close. He has no head covering and wears a toga that is off-white with a burgundy overlay. The holograms of Muhammad and Paul are so realistic that from a distance one can notice no difference between them and Bowers. All conversations have ceased at this point. Very little sound is heard. Tens of thousands of camera flashes go off for a solid minute.

The three make their way to the stage and walk up the steps. Once onstage, Bowers invites Muhammad to sit on his right side and Paul on his left. Then he sits down. He has a pleasant yet commanding manner. He talks briefly with the two men, then stands up and walks to the podium positioned in the front center portion of the stage. The debate has begun.

"Good evening, ladies and gentlemen. This is a historic moment. I think I can safely say that nothing like this has ever taken place in human history. It is as though two prominent historical figures have simultaneously returned to our world in order to explain and argue their particular beliefs. I would like to both thank and commend MIT and the scientists of Project Resurrection for the amazing job they have done! I am neither a Muslim nor a Christian. And yet I cannot help being in complete and indescribable awe of what I see. I am honored to be tonight's moderator.

"Amazing technology allows us to hear these two major leaders share why we should embrace their particular world-view. We can easily misunderstand one another. Thus our hope for this debate is that we all will gain a greater understanding of one another and why we believe as we do. Let me explain our format this evening. The apostle Paul will start with an opening speech, not to exceed twenty-five minutes. The prophet Muhammad will follow with his twenty-five-minute opening speech. We will then hear rebuttals from each. Paul will go first with his rebuttal, not to exceed twenty minutes. This will be followed by Muhammad's rebuttal, also not to exceed twenty minutes.

"We will then transition into a discussion period where I will ask questions of both Muhammad and Paul. My role in this part of the debate will be to serve as a facilitator, as I hope Muhammad and Paul will interact with one another. This discussion period will last about two hours. Finally, Muhammad will be invited to offer a five-minute closing speech. Then I will extend the same invitation to Paul.

"Ladies and gentlemen, as a philosopher I would like to encourage every one of you to analyze their arguments as dispassionately as possible. Recognize that most of us have a strong bias that can block our ability to reason. Seek to understand the other view.

"Our speakers need no introduction. To give them one, I believe, would dishonor them. So, without any further delay, I would now like to invite the apostle Paul to come up and share the Christian position."

Paul stands and walks to the podium. As he does, a hearty applause breaks out from the large number of Christians in attendance. In the interest of peace, some Muslims present who would normally have jeered him sit quietly. Paul looks at the massive audience. He smiles as if pleased to have so many to talk to and begins to speak.

2

Paul's Opening Statement

Grace to you and peace from God the Father and the Lord
Jesus Christ! Through him I am able to come to you this
evening proclaiming his salvation. Now I realize that many
of you in this great stadium and many more who are watching by television are neither Muslim nor Christian. So what
is the relevance of tonight's debate for you? If the foundational teaching of Christianity is true—namely, that Jesus
actually rose from the dead—this signifies God's revelation
of himself to the world, specifically and exclusively, through
Jesus Christ our Lord. Accordingly, in my limited time this
evening, I'm going to focus attention on this event.

For me, Jesus's resurrection from the dead is one of the
most interesting and important topics for discussion. Let
me explain why. Two years after Jesus's crucifixion, I was an
enemy of Christianity. I was a pious Jew, circumcised when
I was eight days old, a Jew from Israel, and a member of
the tribe of Benjamin. In other words, I was as pure a Jew
as one can be. I was a Jew's Jew. I was also a Pharisee. This
group demanded strict obedience to the Jewish law. And

zealous? You bet I was. I harshly persecuted the church. And I obeyed the Jewish law so carefully that I was never accused of any fault.[1] I was one of the most religious Jews of my own age, and I tried as hard as possible to follow all the old traditions of my religion.[2] But then something happened: I had the original Damascus Road experience. I was on my way to Damascus to arrest Christians and bring them back to Jerusalem for trial as lawbreakers. It was around noon when suddenly a bright light, brighter than the sun, shone from heaven. In fear I fell to the ground. Then a voice said to me, "Saul, Saul, why are you persecuting me?" Saul was my Jewish name. I said, "Who are you, Lord?" And he said, "I am Jesus, whom you are persecuting. Get up and enter the city, and it will be told you what you must do."[3]

I did not have to wonder if my experience was the real thing. My traveling companions also saw the light and heard the voice. Moreover, I was blind for a couple of days afterward. So I obeyed him, of course. You can imagine the predicament in which I found myself. My Jewish beliefs did not allow for a dead and resurrected Messiah, and yet this was precisely who confronted me on the road. I couldn't just say, "Lord, it was nice to meet you. Thanks for taking time out of your busy schedule to visit me. But I'm going to go on with my plans because my worldview just does not allow anything different."

This is the reason why Jesus's resurrection is important: the truth of Christianity hinges on it. Jesus's atoning death and subsequent resurrection have been the bedrock doctrines of Christianity since its beginning. If they did not occur, the foundation collapses, and Christianity is false. Thus, if Christ has not been raised, the Christian faith is worthless.[4] However, if Jesus was actually resurrected, then there seems to be good reason for believing that Christianity is true.

Accordingly, if Jesus rose from the dead and your world-view does not allow belief in it, then, like me, you may find it time to change your worldview. That is why this evening's debate is more than just an academic discussion. Our eternal destiny hinges on what we do with Jesus and his resurrection.

My case for the resurrection of Jesus will be based on three facts for which I will present strong evidence. This evidence consists of logical arguments, nonbiblical testimony, and biblical testimony for which a robust case for historicity can be made. Indeed, my three facts can be supported and accepted by the professional historian. This doesn't mean that every historian accepts the facts I'm presenting. However, most do.

So obviously I am not arguing "The Bible says it, I believe it, and that settles it for me." It is more like what Tom Cruise's character said in the movie *A Few Good Men*: "It doesn't matter what I believe. It only matters what I can prove." I would like now to focus on three facts which pertain to the resurrection of Jesus and are strongly evidenced.

Fact number one: Jesus's death by crucifixion. Let me provide four reasons why we can be confident that Jesus experienced death by crucifixion. First, a number of Christian and non-Christian ancient sources report it. In addition to a number of early Christian writings, Josephus, Tacitus, Lucian, and Mara bar Serapion all report the event.

Second, the chances of surviving crucifixion were extremely slim. Crucifixion with the torture that usually preceded it was regarded by many in my day as the worst way to die. Those of you who saw Mel Gibson's movie *The Passion of the Christ* witnessed the brutal practice of scourging. A number of writers from my era described it. Josephus reports of a man who was whipped to the bone about six years after my death.[5] In a second-century text named *The Martyrdom of Polycarp*, the Roman whip is said to expose a person's veins and arteries.[6] The victim was then forced to carry his crossbeam outside the city walls, where soldiers would use nails to impale him to a cross or a tree. Then he was left hanging there in excruciating pain. In fact, your English word *excruciating* comes from the Latin "out of the cross." In the first century, a Roman philosopher named Seneca described crucified victims as being maimed, misshapen, deformed, nailed, and having "difficult breathing amid prolonged torture."[7] Only one account exists of a person surviving crucifixion. Josephus reported seeing three of his friends crucified.[8] He appealed to his friend, the Roman commander Titus, who ordered that all three be removed immediately and provided the best medical care Rome had to offer. In spite of this, two of the three still died. Thus, even if Jesus had been removed prematurely and medically assisted, his chances of survival were pretty bleak. Moreover, we have no evidence that Jesus was removed while alive or that he was provided any medical care whatsoever, much less Rome's best.

Third, professional medical opinions are unanimous in concluding that Jesus certainly died as a result of being crucified.[9] While some debate remains regarding the actual cause of his death by crucifixion, the majority opinion is that he died by asphyxiation—or from a lack of oxygen—and our historical understanding of crucifixion supports that conclusion.[10]

Fourth, the nineteenth-century liberal scholar David Strauss noted that even if Jesus had somehow survived crucifixion, he could not have convinced his disciples that he had been resurrected. Imagine Jesus half dead in the tomb. He revives out of a coma and finds himself scared in the dark. He places his nail-pierced hands on the very heavy stone blocking his exit and pushes it out of the way. Then he's met by the guards, who say, "Hey, maggot, where do you think you're going?" He answers them, "I'm out of this hole." Then he beats them up. He then walks blocks, if not miles, on pierced and wounded feet in order to find his disciples. Finally he comes to the house where they're staying and knocks on the door. Peter opens the door and sees Jesus hunched over in his pathetic and mutilated state and says, "Wow! I can't wait to have a resurrected body just like that!" No, he would have said, "Somebody get a doctor! It's Jesus and he needs help!" Strauss went on to say that there is no way Jesus could have convinced his disciples he was the risen Lord of life. Alive? Barely. Risen? No way.

In summary, we can know that Jesus died by crucifixion because it is multiply attested by both Christian and non-Christian sources; the chances of surviving crucifixion were very bleak; the uniform professional medical opinion is that Jesus died; and Strauss's critique rightly observed that even if Jesus had survived crucifixion, he could not have convinced his disciples in his physical state that he was the risen Lord of life. Even today's highly skeptical co-founder of the Jesus Seminar, John Dominic Crossan, concludes, "That [Jesus] was crucified is as sure as anything historical can ever be."[11] On three occasions in the same book, Crossan affirms that this event resulted in Jesus's death. Thus, given the strong evidence for Jesus's death by crucifixion, without good evidence to the contrary, the historian must conclude that Jesus was crucified and that the process killed him.

Fact number two: the empty tomb. Allow me to provide three reasons why you should believe Jesus's tomb was empty. The first reason is the Jerusalem factor. Jesus had been publicly executed and buried in Jerusalem. Then his resurrection was proclaimed there publicly. So for Christianity to get off the ground in Jerusalem, the body of Jesus could not have been in the tomb. His Roman and Jewish enemies would have only had to visit the tomb and view the corpse and the misunderstanding would have been over. Not only is there not so much as a suggestion that this occurred but their response was quite different.

This brings us to my second argument, and it pertains specifically to that response: Jesus's enemies acknowledged the empty tomb. The ancient authors Justin and Tertullian reported that members of the Jewish leadership were claiming that the disciples of Jesus had stolen his body.[12] This is outside corroboration of a similar report in Matthew 28:13 and seems to be an attempt to account for a missing corpse. This is like the eight-year-old student who tells his teacher that the dog ate his homework. He would not say this if he had it to turn in. Likewise, you would not claim that the body of Jesus had been stolen if it was still in the tomb. Paul Maier, distinguished professor of ancient history at Western Michigan University, writes, "Jewish polemic shared with Christians the conviction that the sepulcher was empty, but gave natural explanations for it. And such positive evidence within a hostile source is the strongest kind of evidence and becomes self-authenticating."[13]

Third, the claim that Jesus had been *resurrected* suggests an empty tomb. People in antiquity held a variety of views of the afterlife. Pagans believed they would be freed from the body and become a disembodied spirit after death. Jews held a couple of views. My Jewish opponents, the Sadducees, did not believe in life after death. Rather they held that when you died, that was it; no heaven. Others, like Josephus and Herod, may have held to a type of re-incarnation. But the majority of Jews held that the body that dies and is buried is the same body that will be raised and transformed into an immortal body.[14] They called this *resurrection*. An example is found in 2 Maccabees 7, where a pagan king brutally tortures and kills seven brothers for their unwillingness to break the Jewish law. While their mother watches, one by one her seven sons have their tongues, hands, and feet cut off before being placed in a large pan and fried to death. Having seen this happen to two of his brothers, the third sticks out his tongue, stretches forth his hands, and tells the king that he hopes to get them back from God. When they come to the fourth brother, he says that he cherishes the hope of resurrection and then goes to the same type of death. Thus the term *resurrection* meant that the *body* would be brought back to life. Even the Qur'an holds to bodily resurrection. In sura 75 we are told that on the last day when the resurrection occurs, Allah will reassemble bones and restore a person down to their very fingertips. Here's the point: If people were claiming that the corpse of Jesus had been resurrected and that he was walking around and showing himself to others, this infers belief in his empty tomb. If they had thought he continued to live in a sort of *spiritual* or immaterial existence, they may have said that Jesus was living, as he had claimed Abraham, Isaac, and Jacob were still living.[15] But they would not have said *resurrection*, a term that referred to bringing the corpse back to life.

So we discover that there is good evidence for the empty tomb: the Jerusalem factor; that it is acknowledged by Jesus's enemies; and that the claim of resurrection infers an empty tomb. William Wand of Oxford writes, "All the strictly historical evidence we have is in favor of [the empty tomb], and those scholars who reject it ought to recognize that they do so on some other ground than that of scientific history."[16]

So here's where we are: we have established that Jesus died by crucifixion and that subsequent to his death his tomb was empty. Now, as some of your television commercials would say, *But wait! There's more!*

Fact number three: the appearances. Something occurred that convinced a number of people, both friend and foe, that Jesus had appeared to them because he had been resurrected.

I'd like to focus on a major passage, a creed found in the fifteenth chapter of my first letter to the church at Corinth. It reads:

> Christ died for our sins according to the Scriptures, and that he was buried, and that he was raised on the third day according to the Scriptures, and that he appeared to Peter, then to the twelve, after that he appeared to more than five hundred followers of Jesus at one time, most of whom are still alive, but some have died, after that he appeared to James, then to all the apostles.

Then I added that Jesus appeared to me too.[17]

Today's scholars date this creed as very early, usually within five years of the crucifixion of Jesus.[18] Jesus's death, burial, resurrection, and five postresurrection appearances were reported. In my letter to the church in Corinth, I added my own name to the list in the creed. A few verses after this creed, I explained that this is what the disciples were teaching[19] and referred to it as *kerygma*,[20] a word we early Christians used to identify our official and formal teaching. A disciple of Peter named Clement of Rome knew the disciples personally and likewise reported that this was what they were teaching.[21] Thus we have two independent sources who personally knew the disciples and reported they were claiming Jesus had been resurrected and had appeared to them. Accordingly, we have what amounts to a certifiably official and formal teaching of the disciples on the resurrection of Jesus.

But we can go further. A number of independent sources in antiquity attest to the disciples' willingness to suffer and even die for this belief.[22] This does not prove their beliefs were true, since people of other faiths are likewise willing to die for their convictions. However, being willing to die for their convictions does indicate that they *believed* they knew the truth. Something happened to make them believe they had seen the risen Jesus—and to believe it so strongly that they were willing to endure great suffering and even death for proclaiming it. Liars make poor martyrs. So we can establish that the original disciples not only claimed the risen Jesus had appeared to them—they really believed it.

It is also very interesting that not only Jesus's *friends* believed he had appeared to them but also an *enemy*: me. Remember that earlier I said I had persecuted Christians. I arrested them, beat them, threw them in prison, and consented to their execution for being Christians. Then I became one because I believed that the risen Jesus had appeared to me. I testified to this in my letters to the churches in Corinth, Galatia, and Philippi.[23] Luke also confirms it in Acts.[24] Moreover, a very early oral tradition that predates the New Testament refers to me and says, "He who persecuted the church now proclaims the faith he once sought to destroy."[25] So you have early witnesses, eyewitnesses, and multiple witnesses to my conversion. Ladies and gentlemen, this is the type of evidence your historians drool over. Furthermore, my sufferings and martyrdom on behalf of the gospel are reported by a number of independent and ancient sources.[26] As with the disciples, this attests to my sincere belief that I had seen the risen Jesus.

May I also add that, in addition to me, the skeptic James, the half brother of Jesus, converted to Christianity shortly after Jesus's crucifixion because he too believed that the risen Jesus had appeared to him. The Gospels report the embarrassing fact that none of Jesus's brothers believed in him during his ministry.[27] It is highly unlikely that a number of Christians would invent such a story that was so embarrassing and potentially hurtful to the early church. Can't you hear early critics of the church saying, "His own brothers didn't believe in him! So why should we?" So you should find it quite interesting when Luke and I later identify James as a leader in the Jerusalem church.[28] Moreover, James's apparent new belief that his brother was the Messiah was so strong that he died as a martyr. Josephus in the first century, Hegesippus in the second century, and Clement of Alexandria in the third century all report this.[29] What best accounts for this change of heart? The answer is found in the early creed in 1 Corinthians that I cited earlier, which states: "then he appeared to James."[30]

So we have seen that we can be historically certain that Jesus's resurrection was believed by his disciples and at least one if not two of his foes. Paula Fredriksen, a critical scholar at Boston University, comments, "The disciples' conviction that they had seen the Risen Christ . . . [is] historical bedrock, facts known past doubting."[31]

Let me wrap this up by building a case for Jesus's resurrection. Tonight I have approached Jesus's resurrection by considering three major historical facts: Jesus's death by crucifixion, the empty tomb, and the beliefs of a number of people, friend and foe alike, that Jesus had been raised from the dead and had appeared to them. These are based on logical arguments, nonbiblical sources, and biblical sources for which a robust case for historicity can be made. I would also like to add that all three facts are widely accepted by today's Christian and skeptical historians alike.

In historical investigation, very rarely can something be concluded with absolute or 100 percent certainty. Because of this, the historian looks for *high probability* and selects the *best* explanation of the known facts. So what about Jesus's resurrection? Certainly it explains all of the facts and does so easily and without strain. But can any *natural* explanation account for them just as well? Can I explain these facts using other theories given what we know from science, history, psychology, or philosophy? No. Not only are these theories unable to account for all of the facts but most of the time the facts themselves serve as refutations of them. For example, the proposal that my colleagues, the disciples, stole the body and lied about the appearances would not account for the conversions of skeptics like James and me. We would have been the first to suspect fraud. Thus, when it comes to Jesus's resurrection, naturalistic theories all fail.

So Muhammad has to show either that I'm wrong on these facts or that the logic of my argument for Jesus's resurrection is flawed. If he decides to present an alternate theory to Jesus's resurrection, he must demonstrate that his theory is at least equally viable to Jesus's resurrection. Unless and until he does this, the resurrection of Jesus is the best explanation of the historical facts, and therefore, we can conclude with confidence that it was an event that occurred in history. And if it did occur, Christianity is true and Islam is false. Thank you.

Paul turns from the podium and begins walking back to his seat. The Christians erupt with a standing ovation. This is about a third of the capacity crowd. Most Muslims remain silent, looking somewhat sheepishly at the Christians around them who are applauding Paul. The applause lasts for two full minutes without signs of stopping. Dr. Sweeney looks over at Dr. Bahkr and says, "This is amazing, Ahmad! Can you believe how good this has turned out?"

"It's very good," he says. But his response is much less sanguine than she expected.

"Is something wrong?" she asks.

"No, no. Nothing's wrong. I want to hear what the prophet Muhammad will say." Bahkr's response surprises Sweeney. She knows he is a Muslim, but he has never spoken of his Islamic faith in front of her. He has obviously been drawn into this debate and somehow views Paul's speech as somewhat of a threat.

Bowers walks to the podium and motions for the crowd to be silent. The applause quickly dies down. He then says, "And now I would like to invite Muhammad to come share the Muslim position." As Muhammad stands up and approaches the podium, a faint sound from a few who applaud is heard. But the sound is lost in an undercurrent of awe and then the sound of twenty thousand or more Muslims standing quickly to their feet in respect. Muhammad smiles with gratification at the gesture, motions for everyone to be seated, and begins to speak.

3

Muhammad's Opening Statement

In the name of Allah, the most gracious, ever merciful. Praise be to Allah, the compassionate, the merciful, creator and sustainer of the universe. And may peace and blessings be upon all of his messengers. I would like to thank all the Muslims who have wished peace upon me. I am thankful to Allah, most gracious, most merciful, for allowing me the opportunity to speak in person to the world about his glorious message. The question that concerns us this evening is *Did Jesus rise from the dead?* It is a wonderful question to ask and I am most delighted and humbled to represent the side of Islam. It is not my own. I am only a prophet. It belongs to Allah. Praised be his name.

I know Islam is true because Allah's angel Gabriel appeared to me not once but many times and gave me, his humble servant, the most glorious word of Allah: the Qur'an. At the time when the angel Gabriel first appeared to me, I was very grieved at the worship of pagan gods by those around me. I was appalled that man, who had been made in Allah's image, would stoop so low as to worship that which Allah created and which was subject to man. I knew this was not pleasing to Allah. So I sought to know the truth.

And Allah, praised be his name, was merciful to show me. Therefore, I know Islam is true apart from and in spite of any of these so-called evidences Paul has presented. I encourage all of you today, if you want to know if the Qur'an which was revealed to me is the word of Allah, then gather all the wisest people you can and try to write a sura[1] that will be as good as any of those you find in the Qur'an.[2] You will quickly discover that this book is and could only be the word of Allah. Praise and glory be to his name.

Now, Paul says that if Jesus, on whom be peace, rose from the dead, Christianity is true and Islam is false. This is one thing on which I can agree with Paul. If he can prove to us tonight that Jesus was resurrected, then of course Christianity is true and Islam is false. The Qur'an teaches that Jesus, peace be upon him, did not die on the cross. So if he did, the Qur'an is wrong and cannot be the word of Allah. But proving that Jesus died and rose from the dead is something that Paul has not done and cannot do. It is impossible, and I will now provide you with many reasons why.

Paul provided what he thinks are three historical facts: Jesus's death by crucifixion, the empty tomb, and the beliefs of others including himself that Jesus had been resurrected. His entire case is linked to these three facts. But they are not facts at all.

Let us look first at Paul's claim that it is a fact that Jesus died as a result of being crucified. He gave us four reasons for how we can know Jesus was dead: one, it is testified by several ancient sources, some of which are non-Christian; two, it is highly unlikely that a person can survive crucifixion; three, the opinion of many medical professionals today is that Jesus, peace be upon him, was dead when he was taken off the cross; and four, if Jesus had survived crucifixion, when his disciples saw all of his wounds, they would not have concluded that he had been resurrected.

I will now read to you what the Qur'an says happened. It is found in the fourth sura, verses 157 and 158. This reads,

> That they said (in boast), "We killed Christ Jesus the son of Mary, the Messenger of Allah"—But they killed him not, nor crucified him, but so it was made to appear to them, and those who differ therein are full of doubts, with no (certain) knowledge, but only conjecture to follow, for of a surety they killed him not—Nay, Allah raised him up unto Himself; and Allah is Exalted in Power, Wise. . . .[3]

There are two major ways of understanding this passage. One way is that Jesus, peace be upon him, was not crucified. Instead, someone was made to look like him and the Romans crucified that person, not Jesus. From the early part of the second century on, some people suspected that Simon of Cyrene who carried the cross of Jesus was mistaken for him and was crucified. If this is true, then it was not Jesus who was crucified. Rather, it was Simon. Many others have suggested that when the Jewish leaders came to arrest Jesus after Judas betrayed him, Allah, praise his name, exacted justice and made Judas look like Jesus so that they took him instead and crucified him.[4] These are *substitution theories*.

A second type of theory holds that Jesus was crucified *but*, while he was hanging on the cross, Allah made it appear he had died, though he had not died in reality. They took him off the cross, thinking he was dead, laid him in a tomb, and Allah, praise his wonderful name, healed him and took him to heaven. Either of these two theories of substitution and rescue are in accordance with the Qur'an and show that the cross very likely did not kill Jesus.

Now, can Paul show us that the Qur'an is wrong? He cannot. And since he cannot show that the Qur'an is wrong on this or any other matter, he cannot say that he has *proved* that Jesus died on the cross. With this in mind, let us also consider his arguments for Jesus's death. First, he said that it is testified by several ancient sources. Yes, it is. But if Allah made it appear that Jesus was dead on the cross, we can understand why others reported that he had died. So this does not prove that Jesus died on the cross. It could just as easily prove that Allah, praised be his name, was successful in misleading those who were trying to kill Jesus.

Paul's second argument is that it is very unlikely that a person could survive crucifixion. I agree—but it is also very unlikely that a person could rise from the dead! If Allah, praised be his name, can raise someone from the dead, then it should be even easier for him to make someone only appear to be dead and then to heal him. Is anything too hard for Allah? I think not.

Paul's third argument is that many contemporary medical professionals hold the opinion that Jesus died on the cross. But it could be that the man made to look like Jesus had these things done to him and died. Scholars have also pointed out that the very medical studies Paul appealed to are horribly unreliable. Medical studies assume that the description of Jesus's crucifixion in the New Testament is accurate. These medical doctors have misinterpreted descriptions meant solely for theological purposes as though they actually occurred. For example, the Gospel of John reports that Jesus was stabbed with a spear that caused blood and water to flow from his body, thus ensuring he was dead.[5]

But the problems with this conclusion are numerous. John is the only Gospel writer who reports it. If this spear wound actually occurred, why didn't any of the other Gospels report it? Since John is the last of the four Gospels to have been written, and since none of the others mention it, legend is a very good candidate for the origin of the story. Moreover, many theologians agree that the blood and water are theological terms that are used elsewhere in the New Testament and were used by John for theological rather than historical purposes. For example, in 1 John 5:6 and 8, John says about Jesus, "This is the one who came by water and blood, Jesus Christ; not with the water only, but with the water and with the blood" and "the Spirit and the water and the blood; and these three are one." Notice it is the same author, John, who is writing these. But there are even more problems. In antiquity, no accurate medical tests like EKGs and EEGs existed to ensure a person was dead. Even in the twentieth century, people were declared dead only to be revived. So how could anyone be certain Jesus was dead when they removed him from the cross, assuming it was him rather than a substitute?

Furthermore, crucifixion was not a short ordeal. People could last for days on the cross. But the Gospels report that Jesus was dead within six hours. This casts doubt on whether Jesus actually died. Why would everyone else last so long and yet the one whom Christians believe to be the Son of God last only six hours? This is especially problematic if Jesus was dying for the sins of the world as Paul believes. If this was the case, we would expect him to live on the cross for perhaps weeks! If Jesus was indeed crucified, the fact that people thought he was dead after only six hours supports the Qur'an's view of what happened to Jesus more than it does the view presented in the New Testament.

Because of this we can understand why the Gospels also report that Pilate was amazed upon hearing that Jesus had died so quickly.[6] It is as though he was suspicious of something. But what could that something have been? We can only speculate here. The Gospels report that Pilate did not want to have Jesus crucified. If the Gospels are telling the truth on this matter, Pilate made repeated attempts to set him free.[7] When the centurion witnessed Jesus's death, he said that Jesus was the Son of God.[8] He appears to have been a Christian, does he not? Would a Christian kill his Lord? Why not save his Lord and please his earthly boss all at the same time? Pilate's desire to free Jesus and the Christian centurion's likely unwillingness to kill his Lord provide good reason to doubt Jesus's death on the cross. Thus, the Gospel accounts of what happened to Jesus are once again more in line with what the Qur'an says occurred than with the idea that Jesus actually died.

What about Paul's fourth reason why we all can be certain that Jesus died? He gave us the critique of David Strauss. Strauss wrote that if Jesus did not really die on the cross and was able somehow to get out of the tomb and find his disciples, they would not have believed he had been resurrected in an immortal and glorious body, given his terribly wounded body. I agree with Paul here. But this does not weaken our confidence in the Qur'an. If Allah substituted someone for Jesus at his arrest, then Jesus would have appeared totally healthy to his disciples if he later appeared to them. If Allah rescued Jesus from death and healed him, then again, he would have appeared totally healthy to his disciples if he later appeared to them. Strauss's critique is impotent.

So we see many reasons for doubting Paul's first fact that Jesus died as a result of being crucified. Please hear me on this: as long as there is a sufficient amount of doubt regarding Jesus's death, one can never be confident that the eyewitnesses actually saw the risen Jesus. After all, you cannot have a resurrection unless you have a death. However, you can have a rescue, as the Qur'an reports.

Let us move on now to Paul's second point: the empty tomb. He says we can be very confident that the tomb was empty on Sunday morning. He gave us three reasons for believing this: one, if the body of Jesus still lay in the tomb, the enemies of Jesus would have exposed it to show

(44)

he had not been raised; two, Jesus's enemies acknowledged the empty tomb; and three, since the definition of resurrection involves bringing the corpse back to life, the early Christians must have known about the empty tomb. Based on these three reasons, he concludes that the tomb must have been empty.

I find several problems with what he calls "evidence." For one, the empty tomb account is probably a legendary story that was invented years after Jesus's crucifixion. The first time it is mentioned is in the Gospel of Mark, the writing of which is dated by critics at around forty years after Jesus. That is a long time for stories to develop.

Notice that the earliest New Testament author, who is none other than Paul himself, never mentioned the empty tomb in his writings; not even in his famous chapter on resurrection, 1 Corinthians 15. Why not, Paul? If you had known about it, you would have mentioned it. You wrote 1 Corinthians around the year 57, if I am correct. It seems that the empty tomb wasn't known then. Only when we read Mark's Gospel, which was written more than a decade later, do we hear of the empty tomb.

The contemporary New Testament scholar John Dominic Crossan believes the empty tomb is a legend. He notes that typically the victim of crucifixion was left on the cross for some time even after he had died in order for his body to be devoured by scavengers such as dogs, birds, and insects. After these had done their job, what was left of the corpse would be thrown into a common pit.[9] Therefore, the specific location of the body of Jesus, assuming the corpse was the body of Jesus rather than the corpse of Judas or Simon of Cyrene, would not have been known to early Christians. His leg here. His arm somewhere else. Who knows where? An empty tomb story would need to be invented.

Even if Jesus had been buried in a tomb, there is also the possibility that his followers went to the wrong tomb, saw that it was empty, and proclaimed that he had been resurrected. Why should we believe the Gospels anyway? Their authors were obviously biased. They contradict one another a number of times, even in the accounts of the resurrection itself! For example, Mark and Luke report that a man met the women at the tomb, whereas Matthew and John call it an angel. Matthew and Mark say it was one person, whereas Luke and John say there were two. So which is it? Angelic or human? One or two? Both cannot be true.

Look very carefully at what is happening with the reports in the Gospels concerning Jesus's resurrection. No appearances are reported in Mark, the earliest of the Gospels. The appearances aren't reported until the next Gospel, which was either Matthew or Luke. Then notice what happens. We go from a single young man in Mark to an angel in Matthew to two angels in Luke and John. An evolution of the story is occurring right before our eyes. Even worse is that many scholars, including one of Christianity's great scholars, Raymond Brown, believe these angels are not real at all but were later added to the story. This was a common rhetorical practice.[10] So some of what was reported concerning Jesus's resurrection was not intended to be understood literally. Therefore, given the facts that the empty tomb does not appear in the earliest records, that biases and contradictions exist, and that the accounts were gradually embellished and many times were not meant to be understood literally, we should not believe that Jesus's tomb was empty on the Sunday morning after his crucifixion.

Before we move on to Paul's third fact, let me add one more thing that settles the matter. I think I have provided enough refutations to Paul's view. But I'll go well beyond what is required. Let us suppose for a moment that the second interpretation of sura 4, verses 157 and 158, in the Qur'an is true. Allah permitted Jesus to be crucified. After a few hours he made it appear as though Jesus had died. The guards removed Jesus from the cross, and he was buried. Allah then healed him and restored him to health. He showed himself later to his disciples, who thought he had been resurrected because they thought he had died. Had they known at that moment what Allah had done, they would not have used the term *resurrection*. This explanation acknowledges the empty tomb and even acknowledges that Allah was the cause of its emptiness. Therefore, the empty tomb is just as easily explained by the Qur'an as it is by the New Testament. The difference is that the Qur'an does not suffer from all of the problems I have shown that the New Testament is plagued by. So this entire issue is a moot point. The tomb may or may not have been empty. However, even if it was, we have no reason to conclude that Allah performed a *resurrection* on Jesus, peace be upon him. And Paul's entire argument for Christianity and against Islam is not that Jesus was seen alive after a crucifixion. It is specifically that he was *resurrected*.

We now arrive at Paul's third fact: the appearances. We saw just a few moments ago that even if these appearances really occurred, we have no way to be confident that they were resurrection appearances. *If* they actually happened, one of two scenarios seems more likely: Jesus, on whom be peace, was either substituted or rescued. If Allah provided a substitution, Jesus, on whom be peace, was not crucified and later showed himself to others. If he was rescued by Allah, then he was crucified, removed prior to dying, and restored to complete health by Allah, and he later showed himself to others. My point is this: even if the appearances occurred, they present no problem for Muslims.

But let us look for a moment at Paul's evidence and ask whether it is sufficient. He started by appealing to *kerygma* that speaks of Jesus's resurrection. He provided one example from 1 Corinthians 15, verses 3–7. This is from a letter that you wrote, Paul! It is not distinct from you. For all we know, *you* invented that creed.

(47)

Paul then noted that he and Clement of Rome knew the disciples and had reported they were claiming Jesus had been resurrected. The problem with this is that Clement of Rome is later than Matthew, Mark, and Luke, who are already late. So he may have just copied from what they wrote in the Gospels. Paul, you are the earliest, and I am quite confident that you invented the Christianity we know today. Jesus, peace be upon him, would not approve of what you did to his teachings. You claimed Jesus is the Son of God, and even God![11] But Jesus never claimed that of himself. Never do we find, even in the Gospels, Jesus saying, "I am God!" In fact, he denies such a claim in the Qur'an. It is written:

> And behold! Allah will say: "O Jesus the son of Mary! Didst thou say unto men, 'Worship me and my mother as gods in derogation of Allah'?" He will say: "Glory to Thee! Never could I say what I had no right (to say). Had I said such a thing, Thou wouldst indeed have known it. Thou knowest what is in my heart, though I know not what is in Thine. For Thou knowest in full all that is hidden."[12]

It is likewise written:

> O People of the Book! Commit no excesses in your religion: nor say of Allah aught but the truth. Christ Jesus the son of Mary was (no more than) a Messenger of Allah, and His Word, which He bestowed on Mary, and a Spirit proceeding from Him: so believe in Allah and his Messengers. Say not "Trinity": desist: It will be better for you: for Allah is One God: Glory be to Him: (Far Exalted is He) above having a son. To Him belong all things in the heavens and on earth. And enough is Allah as a Disposer of affairs.[13]

Paul, if you'll invent such blasphemous doctrines as that Jesus is God, why should we believe you on anything you tell us? You have only provided two sources: Clement who is very late and you who invented Christianity. This is the extent of your argument, is it not?

But there are even more problems with your claim. Another problem is that according to Acts 10:39–41, Jesus only appeared to those whom God chose beforehand. How convenient. Why not appear to many others if he wanted the whole world to know?

Still another problem is that even when Jesus allegedly appeared to his disciples, the Gospel of Matthew reports that several of them doubted it was him. Doesn't this sound more like a hallucination or a delusion? The Gospel of Luke reports that Jesus appeared to two of his disciples, although not two of the twelve, along the road to Emmaus. But they didn't recognize him. When they finally did recognize him, he disappeared. Again, doesn't this sound more like a hallucination or a delusion? I could say so much more here, but I am out of time. Nevertheless, what I have said has refuted Paul ten times over. I can provide much more later in the debate if Paul would like.

Now I will conclude. Paul claimed that Christianity is true and Islam is false because he knows that Jesus rose from the dead. As evidence for the resurrection of Jesus, upon whom be peace, he gave three facts: the death of Jesus by crucifixion, the empty tomb, and the appearances. But I have shown that these are not facts at all. Rather, they are beliefs that have many, many, many problems. Thus, Paul's evidence fails. But again, I will go even further and beyond what is required so that you will have no doubt as to who is telling the truth. He said that there are no natural explanations that can account for his three facts. But I have shown that there are several, such as legend, lies, and that the wrong tomb may have been visited, to name just a few. Even worse for Paul is that I do not have to provide any natural explanations, since even if the second and third of Paul's facts are true, this does not lead us to conclude that Jesus rose. The Qur'an provides a different explanation that is supernatural and is the true account of what happened to Jesus.

So there is no reason for believing that Jesus rose from the dead and thus no reason for believing that Christianity is true. On the other hand, we have seen that there is good reason to believe Islam is true, since I am an eyewitness to the revelation of Allah's glorious Qur'an. Furthermore, the Qur'an is so marvelous that no one but Allah could have produced it. Praise be to Allah, most merciful and compassionate.

Muhammad steps backward, turns around, and returns to his seat. The crowd of sixty thousand is completely silent for several long seconds until a lone Muslim shouts loudly in Arabic: "Ashadu la illaha il Allah, wa Muhammadur rasul Allah!" *This is the Shahada, and translated it means, "There is no God but Allah, and Muhammad is his prophet." At this there is an explosion of noise as every Muslim present repeats the Shahada as though in a single voice:* "Ashadu la illaha il Allah, wa Muhammadur rasul Allah!"

Bowers sits stunned at this awe-inspiring moment. Dr. Sweeney looks over at Dr. Bahkr, who is smiling and nodding, his lips moving ever so slightly as if reciting the Shahada with the rest. Sweeney had never given religion much thought. She was not hostile to the thought of God. She simply did not give it any thought at all. To her, religion hardly seemed relevant in an age of science. However, she now sees Bahkr's interest and has to admit to herself that the historical arguments can be quite rational and compelling.

The chant continues for nearly two and a half minutes until Bowers approaches the podium and announces, "Paul will now have twenty minutes for his rebuttal." An uncomfortable silence falls as Paul comes to the podium. He looks around as before and smiles. His face has a countenance of peace and confidence.

4

Paul's Rebuttal

If Muhammad is correct in his facts, then much of what he just said in his opening speech would demolish my argument for Christianity, I admit. However, he is terribly inaccurate in most of what he stated. Since I have been provided only twenty minutes in which to respond, I cannot possibly address all of his arguments in detail within my rebuttal. Therefore, I will categorize his objections to Jesus's resurrection and address the categories as they pertain to the three facts I provided. If Muhammad would like to follow up on any specific topics, I will be happy to address them in our discussion period.

The first category concerns Muhammad's claims against the Gospels. He said many things: that they were written too late, that they contradict one another, that we can see the development of legend occurring right before our eyes, and that their authors were biased. Thus he concludes that we cannot trust their accounts of Jesus's resurrection. I disagree completely with both his assertions against the Gospels and his conclusion. I wish that I had the time needed to address these.[1] However, it is completely unnecessary, since I never appealed to the Gospels as evidence for Jesus's resurrection.

I realize that many of today's skeptical scholars are critical of the Gospels. That is why I took the approach of only considering facts about Jesus that we can prove with a high degree of historical certainty. Remember that the three facts I provided are strongly evidenced and acknowledged by an impressive majority of today's scholars, including skeptical ones. Therefore, even if virtually everything Muhammad said about the Gospels is true—and I assure you it is not—it would not have much power against my case for Christianity. He is using what is called a straw man argument. He is attacking arguments I never gave and then saying he has refuted my position. It is as though Muhammad is attacking a hill. He's throwing spears, arrows, and fire bombs; we hear a lot of noise and see a lot of smoke. But I'm over here on this other hill watching it all happen and thinking, *What is he doing? I'm on this other hill. Is he afraid to confront the facts directly? Come on! Give me your best shot!* Muhammad was very articulate in his opening speech. Unfortunately for him, not only is he incorrect on the majority of it but, even worse, nearly all of it is irrelevant to our debate this evening.

Let's look now at some other things he claimed that were aimed directly at my three facts. Regarding Jesus's death by crucifixion, he said that we cannot be certain his death actually occurred. He cited the Qur'an and said that if its account of what happened to Jesus is true, then the fact that some wrote of Jesus's death should not seem surprising to us, since this indicates that Allah was successful in making it *appear* that Jesus had died when he had not. What we did not hear from Muhammad was genuine evidence that the Qur'an is true. He claims it was delivered to him by an angel. But Joseph Smith claimed that the Book of

Mormon was delivered to him by an angel, too. Should we believe Smith? Only if we can test what is in the book and can verify its accuracy. Unfortunately for Mormons, the evidence is not in their favor.[2] What is Muhammad's test for knowing that the Qur'an is from Allah? He points to the test provided by the Qur'an: assemble all of the wisest people in the world and try to write a sura comparable to one in the Qur'an. When we find that this cannot be done because of the superiority of the Qur'an, we will know that it has a divine origin. I accepted this challenge. I took the first sura and, since I am not an artist, rather than attempt to write my own, I searched for something already in print that could be compared with it. I found Psalm 19.

In sura 1, Allah is praised; he is called the most gracious and merciful, the cherisher and sustainer of the world, and master of the Day of Judgment. It goes on to say that we worship Allah and ask for his help and for him to show us the correct path on which to walk.

When we come to Psalm 19, we also find God praised. The heavens and skies that he created declare his glory in every language. God's law, statutes, precepts, commands, and ordinances and our fear of him are all good and relevant for our lives. The psalm goes on to say that we ask him to forgive us and keep us from sinning. We want our words and thoughts to be pleasing to God.

These two passages contain almost identical messages. However, Psalm 19 does so in a manner that is much more pregnant with meaning and beauty. Now, Muhammad may wish to counter by claiming that the Qur'an must be read in Arabic in order for its full beauty to be understood and that there is a beautiful rhythm to the Qur'an noticed only when read properly in Arabic. But has he read the psalms in Hebrew? Psalms are actually songs, and they have a rhythm to them in Hebrew that is not perceived in other languages. Thus this seems to come down to the matter of which language one prefers as the more beautiful. I think Psalm 19 is superior to sura 1 in both its content and beauty. So I have completed the test the Qur'an provides to judge whether it came from Allah—and the Qur'an has failed. It is not a good test anyway, since literary beauty is a matter of personal preference on which people differ.[3]

Now, since the Qur'an has failed its own test, Muhammad's argument from the Qur'an 4:157–158, that Allah made it only appear that Jesus had died on the cross, is impotent. But there is another reason for believing Jesus died that Muhammad should consider. In addition to all of the historical evidence I presented earlier, if Jesus did not die a violent death on the cross, he is a false prophet.

The tradition that Jesus predicted his death can be traced to very close to if not to the time of Jesus, eliminating the theory that the traditions were invented much later. The earliest Gospel, which is Mark, portrays Jesus predicting his violent death on five occasions. Four of these are likewise reported by Matthew and Luke, and the fifth is also reported by Matthew.[4] They also appear in multiple literary forms, which indicates an even earlier origin, since historians agree that invented things do not appear first in multiple forms. For example, in Mark 10:33–34, Jesus predicted his violent death in straightforward terms:

> Behold, we are going to Jerusalem, and the Son of Man will be delivered to the chief priests and scribes; and they will condemn him to death and deliver him to the Gentiles. And they will mock him and spit on him and scourge him and kill him, and after three days he will rise.

However, in Mark 12:1–11 he predicts his violent death using a parable. In this story an absentee landlord leases his vineyard to farmers. When the time comes for the farmers to pay the landlord, a number of servants are sent to collect.

But they are beaten or killed. The landlord finally sends his son, whom they also kill. In this parable the landlord is God, the vineyard is Israel, the farmers are the Jewish leaders, the servants are the prophets, and the son is Jesus.

Even many highly skeptical scholars such as those of the Jesus Seminar believe it is probable that Jesus actually told this parable.[5] This is noteworthy because it is like the old Mikey and Life cereal television commercial. Mikey is a very picky eater and does not like anything. When his brothers put a bowl of Life cereal in front of him, he eats it and likes it. The point made in the commercial is that if even Mikey likes it, the taste must be very good.

The Jesus Seminar rejects a very large majority of what the New Testament attributes as the words of Jesus. They are like the Mikey of scholarship; they don't like anything Jesus said. The fact that they hold that Jesus probably uttered the parable of the vineyard indicates that the evidence for its authenticity must be pretty good. So not only is the tradition early, it probably goes back to Jesus himself.

Now, why is this important? Since Jesus predicted his violent death and Muhammad regards him as a prophet, if Jesus did not die a violent death, that makes him a false prophet, a fact that would be anathema to both Christians and Muslims. Thus, the argument looks like this:

1. Jesus predicted his violent death.
2. If Jesus died a violent death, the Qur'an is wrong, since it claims he escaped death by crucifixion.
3. If Jesus did not die a violent death, the Qur'an is again wrong, since it regards Jesus as a prophet and if he did not die as he predicted, he would be a false prophet.

Either way, the Qur'an is wrong. Let me remind you that in my opening speech I said that my approach was not going to be "The Bible says it, I believe it, and that settles it for me." Rather, this evening I am only presenting what I can prove with a high degree of historical certainty. In light of this, we can see that Muhammad is doing precisely the opposite. He is saying that the Qur'an says it, he believes it, and that settles it for him. The problem with that is, as we have observed, that the Qur'an provides us with no reliable way of knowing whether it is from Allah. The only test it does provide is not very good, and the Qur'an fails it.

Muhammad then said he distrusts the opinion expressed by a number of medical professionals that Jesus could not have survived crucifixion. He says they often confuse portions of the New Testament that were written solely for theological purposes with other portions that are attempts to report history. For example, he cites the spear wound reported by John. He complains that John is the only Gospel to report it and it is the latest of the four. That is correct. But John appears to have been more attentive to detail than the others. For example, historians are quite confident that nails were generally used by the Romans to crucify a victim, rather than binding them to the cross with ropes. Fourteen ancient authors mention nailing, whereas only one mentions binding with ropes. But that source adds that binding was an Egyptian practice.[6] Moreover, when the skeletal remains of a crucified victim were discovered in Jerusalem in 1968, one of the victim's ankles still had a crucifixion nail stuck through it.[7] Thus, without even considering what the Gospels report, it is highly probable that nails were used to affix Jesus to his cross. Yet John is the only Gospel to mention nails.[8]

Two ancient sources outside of the Gospels also mention the Roman practice of *crurifragium*, the breaking of the legs in order to expedite death on the cross.[9] According to Josephus, a first-century historian, Jerusalem Jews were careful to remove victims from their crosses by sunset.[10]

There goes Crossan's view, which Muhammad mentioned, that Jesus was left on the cross long afterward for scavengers to feast off of his corpse. True, the typical Roman practice was to leave the corpse on the cross for a while. But, as Josephus states, Jerusalem was an exception.[11] So, again, it is highly probable that this action of removing Jesus and the two criminals crucified with him from their crosses before sunset would have been planned for Jesus as John reports.[12] Yet, again, John is the only Gospel that mentions the breaking of legs being performed on those crucified with Jesus.

Should we be surprised, then, that he is also the only one to mention the use of a spear with Jesus? He reports that when the soldiers went to expedite Jesus's death by breaking his legs, they noticed he was already dead. At that point, one of the soldiers took a spear and jabbed Jesus in the side. Why do this? Another historian from the first century named Quintilian provided insight when he wrote, "As for those who die on the cross, the executioner does not forbid the burying of those who have been pierced."[13] When watching a movie like *Gladiator* or *Braveheart*, you see the victors going around with their swords, piercing fallen enemies to ensure they are dead. This is what Quintilian was saying the executioner could do with the crucified who had already died. Thus, John's report is in line with how crucifixions were conducted. Accordingly, although he is the only author to report nails, the *crurifragium*, and the spear, we have no reason to doubt his report pertaining to Jesus on these matters. In fact, these are likely.

Muhammad also argued that since those in antiquity did not have sophisticated medical equipment in order to make an accurate pronouncement of death, there is a good chance they were mistaken in thinking Jesus was dead. While it is true that some people in antiquity may have been misdiagnosed for dead, in many instances this would not be a challenge. For example, Roman soldiers would not have needed a modern EKG in order to determine if someone they had just beheaded was really dead. This is where an understanding of the cause of death by crucifixion is helpful. The majority opinion of the professional medical community on death by crucifixion is that the victim died by asphyxiation, which is having not enough oxygen and too much carbon dioxide in the blood. While on the cross, the victim would take as much weight as possible off of his pierced feet by slumping on the cross. In this position, the up-stretched arms would make exhaling difficult. Breathing would become very shallow and difficult. The victim would push up on his pierced feet in order to exhale and get sufficient oxygen, then return to the slumped position. Without being able to exhale, the victim would experience a lack of oxygen and too much carbon dioxide buildup in the blood and would die of asphyxiation, which would be very painful. When the soldiers broke the victim's legs, he could not push up and would die shortly thereafter. Therefore, executioners could very easily know when a victim was dead: he was not pushing up for air.

Muhammad also said John was the last of the Gospels to be written and therefore is suspect of containing legend. He said that the blood and water that John reports flowed as a result of the spear wound is a good example. However, I have shown that the spear wound is likely, and the blood and water can be explained medically. For example, if Jesus had taken a heavy blow to his midsection, his lungs could have filled with fluid as a result.[14] The spear could have punctured a lung and caused blood and water to exit. Even if John had a theological motif in mind in mentioning the blood and water, this does not mean that he invented the blood and water flowing from Jesus. John saw theological significance in the soldiers casting lots for Jesus's clothes, that he was thirsty while on the cross, and that his legs were not broken.[15] This does not mean that he invented all of these. It does not even suggest it.

Therefore, Muhammad's reasons for rejecting the nearly universal professional medical opinion that Jesus died as a result of being crucified are weak. I wish that I had more time to address some of the other things he raised pertaining to Jesus's death. If he thinks they are important, perhaps he can raise them again in our discussion period. In the meantime, I think it is clear: no good reasons exist for doubting Jesus's death by crucifixion. We may not be able to have 100 percent certainty. But we rarely have that much certainty about anything. We can have a very high degree of historical certainty that Jesus was crucified and that he died while on the cross. Appealing to the Qur'an is not a good argument against it. The Qur'an was written six hundred years after Jesus, is fifth-hand testimony at best, and, as we have observed, has many problems on the matter of Jesus's death by crucifixion—specifically, it flies in the face of the strong historical evidence in favor of his death by crucifixion, and it portrays Jesus as a false prophet. No professional historian would accept such weak evidence as a reason for ignoring all of the good evidence to the contrary. Do not be deceived! Jesus was crucified, and the process killed him.

Regarding the empty tomb, Muhammad made a few suggestions as to what he thinks actually occurred. First, he claimed the empty tomb is a legend. He said that I never mentioned the empty tomb in my letters to the churches and that if I were aware of Jesus's empty tomb, I would certainly have mentioned it in the fifteenth chapter of my first letter to the Corinthian church. This is nonsense. I said *resurrection*. How much do I need to spell this out? Today, if a child died of SIDS, the parents would not need to make a point of an empty crib. It is implied.[16] As I shared in my opening speech, the Jewish and Christian concept of resurrection in the first century was the same as the Islamic view of resurrection. It is a bodily event. So if the body that died and is buried is the same body that is raised and seen walking around, this implies an empty tomb. Everyone in my day knew this, just like they knew nails were used in crucifixions. A redundant explanation was not required.

Muhammad then suggested the possibility that the followers of Jesus went to the wrong tomb, discovered it empty, and thought Jesus had been raised. How foolish! Had this been the case, don't you think the Roman and Jewish authorities who had Jesus put to death would have checked the tomb? That certainly would have settled the misunderstanding. Moreover, let us suppose that a modern leader of a religion opposed to yours dies, and within a few days his corpse is reported to have disappeared from the morgue. Would you change your religious beliefs, or would you be more inclined to believe that the corpse had been stolen or misplaced? Ladies and gentlemen, I was a very pious and zealous Jew, as was my colleague James, the half brother of Jesus. Hearing about an empty tomb only made us think that the body had been stolen. The appearance of Jesus to each of us was what convinced us he had been raised from the dead. The empty tomb did not convince us. But it was consistent with the claims that Jesus had been resurrected. Therefore, Muhammad's wrong-tomb theory does not work. It cannot account for the known facts.

So here's where we are: I have established with a high degree of historical certainty that Jesus died on the cross and that his tomb was later discovered to be empty. Moreover, we have seen that none of Muhammad's arguments against these two facts work—not even his suggestion that the tomb was empty because God rescued rather than resurrected

Jesus, since we have no evidence for it. Nothing destroys an otherwise interesting argument like the facts.

What about Muhammad's attacks on my third fact, the appearances? He first said that these can just as easily be explained by the Qur'an as a substitution or rescue. Remember, however, that the Qur'an failed its own test and is demonstrably wrong in the passage regarding the death of Jesus. So that argument fails. Muhammad then challenged the testimonies of Clement and myself that the original disciples were claiming Jesus had been resurrected. He accused Clement of copying from the Gospels. But why would he have to do this if he had heard directly from the disciples? Is it really a big deal that he is writing after them? The apostle John is believed to have lived to the end of the first century and written around the same time as Clement.

Muhammad then accused me of inventing Christianity as it is known today. Oh, I wish that I had time to deal with this now! I will certainly bring it up in the discussion period. For now, I should say that the view that I practically invented Christianity has been largely abandoned by scholars since the end of the 1970s.[17] There are good reasons for that, Muhammad.

In conclusion, we have seen that even after numerous attacks by Muhammad, my three facts stand: Jesus's death by crucifixion, the empty tomb, and the appearances. We have also observed that his arguments for the truth of Islam fail. His position lacks evidence on which we can rely, and when the Qur'an's claim that Jesus did not die is confronted by the strong historical evidence that Jesus predicted his violent death, the Qur'an ends up rendering Jesus as a false prophet in contradiction to Islamic doctrine that honors Jesus as a great prophet. Therefore, the evidence points to Jesus's resurrection from the dead, and thus Christianity is true.

Paul sits down and the nearly twenty thousand Christians present stand to their feet once again with a thunderous applause. After allowing this for about a minute, Bowers walks up to the podium and says, "Muhammad will now share his rebuttal." The equally large Muslim crowd now stands to their feet and applauds Muhammad as he walks up to the podium. Their applause is slightly louder, as though a sort of competition regarding the applause level is taking place at this point.

Dr. Bahkr and Dr. Sweeney are amazed with the results of their work. Bahkr leans toward Sweeney and says, "The presentations of Paul and Muhammad have been nothing short of stunning. I'm so thrilled at how the crowd is completely captivated by them!" At that moment, Muhammad lifts his right hand, asking his followers to become silent and be seated. They do, and he begins speaking.

5

Muhammad's Rebuttal

I was glad to hear Paul admit that if I am correct with my facts, Islam is true and Christianity is false. I know that I am correct in these facts. So I know that today's Christianity is a false religion. Now let us talk about Paul's "facts."

Paul claims that the majority of scholars believe his three facts. This is how he argues, is it not? Paul, I do not care what the majority of scholars believe. Scholars are many times wrong. What they believed one hundred years ago is no longer believed today. Besides, what if we had asked the majority of scholars in the middle of the first century when you were alive whether they believed in the resurrection of Jesus, peace be upon him? Would you want us to believe as the majority of scholars then? I think not. What if we asked a majority of scholars today whether they think Jesus was resurrected? Would you want us to believe as the majority of today's scholars do? The majority of scholars in the first century as well as today would all say that they don't believe Jesus rose from the dead. So let us not toy any longer with such an argument.

Paul attacked the credibility of the Qur'an. I cringed inside when I heard his blasphemous attacks. He said that the claim of an angelic source for the Qur'an is no different than Mormon claims that an angel appeared to Joseph Smith. I do not know what happened with Joseph Smith. Maybe he really did see something. Maybe it was a jinn of an evil sort, or what you call a demon. These can deceive. How do I know that it was not an evil jinn who came to me? I look at the result: a Qur'an which no one can replicate. Paul claims that this is a bad test and that Psalm 19 is better than the first sura. That is Paul's opinion. But I am not concerned with his opinion either. Paul is a blasphemer who said Jesus is the Son of God. He even thinks Jesus is God! Jesus, peace be upon him, never made such claims. In fact, the Qur'an reports Jesus denying that he had made these claims.[1] I made all of these points in my opening statement, and, Paul, you never responded.

You said you did not invent Christianity. But you did. I draw our attention to how you answered my charge that you invented Christianity as it is taught today. You said that the majority of scholars no longer believe this. Is this a good answer? I think not. Paul, you need to prove to us that you did not invent Christianity, not just deny it.

Now, Paul said that he proved the Qur'an to be wrong on the matter of Jesus's death because he thinks the historical method can prove that Jesus predicted his violent death. So if Jesus did not die, he is a false prophet. I would like to discuss this claim for a moment. First, I would like to point out that being a prophet does not mean that the prophet must be 100 percent correct regarding everything that prophet says and thinks. The Jewish and Christian Scriptures of the Old Testament clearly portray Abraham deceiving the king, while just a few verses later God calls Abraham a prophet.[2] How can it be then that a prophet must be telling the truth in everything he says? If that is the case, then your Jewish and Christian God is a liar, since he called the liar Abraham a prophet. The actual test is that if a man who claims to be a prophet is proclaiming a message that he believes he received from God and that message turns out to be wrong, that man is a false prophet. However, if Jesus *believed* he was going to die a violent death and was unaware that Allah would rescue him from dying on the cross, that does not make him a false prophet under anyone's understanding. Jesus's saying, "I think I'm going to die a violent death," is quite different than his saying, "Thus says the Lord: I am going to die a violent death." The former is non-prophetic, whereas the latter is prophetic.

Second, it is not true that Jesus predicted his violent death. One passage frequently appealed to by Christians is the sign of Jonah in Matthew 12:39–40, where Jesus is predicting that as Jonah was in the belly of the great fish for three days and three nights, so will the Son of Man be in the heart of the earth.

Notice first that Jesus refers to himself here as the "Son of Man," emphasizing his humanity, not his divinity, as Paul thinks. Jonah also did not die in the fish, which supports a rescue theory more than it does a resurrection. But most important for the moment is that if Jesus said this at all, he said that he would be in the earth for three days and three nights. This is very interesting! How long do these same Gospels, even Matthew who reports this prediction, say that Jesus was in the tomb? He is buried Friday afternoon. He is still in the tomb twenty-four hours later. But within twelve hours after that, he is gone and the tomb is empty. It is one day and two nights, not three days and three nights. So the same author who reports Jesus's sign of Jonah prediction, Matthew, also reports that it does not come true. Which book is presenting Jesus as a false prophet?

Do you see why I don't believe the Gospels when they claim that Jesus rose from the dead? Not only do they contradict one another but I have just shown how according to Matthew, Jesus is a false prophet. Without Jesus predicting his violent death, Paul's challenge to the Qur'an is demolished, and therefore, we can believe it regarding how Allah kept Jesus, peace be upon him, from being killed on the cross. I never doubted the Qur'an anyway, since I know it is from Allah, most merciful and compassionate. But I realize that it is sometimes necessary to demonstrate through logic that deceivers like Paul are out to lead people away from the truth. So, Paul, I have an argument that works a lot like yours: if Jesus predicted his death as you say, he is a false prophet, since he did not rise in the time he said he would. In this case, you are wrong and Christianity is false. On the other hand, if Jesus did not predict his death, then you have no argument against the Qur'an and again you are wrong. Either way you are wrong, Paul.

Paul then says that I am not using evidence to argue for the truth of Islam. Instead I'm saying that because the Qur'an says it, I believe it and live my life accordingly. That is not completely true. Yes, I believe the Qur'an, and I live my life completely in accordance with all that Allah revealed in it to me. I do not apologize for this. I know that every word of the Qur'an is from Allah! But I also believe that it can be proven that the Qur'an is from Allah. The test mentioned in the Qur'an proves that it is from Allah. Paul attacked it. I showed that he is wrong. But let me add one more thing. Although not provided as a test in the Qur'an, it contains many scientific statements which modern science has confirmed.[3] And yet no one but Allah could have known these things in the seventh century when Allah, the merciful and compassionate, gave it to mankind.

But I'll refrain from providing these, since Paul would only tell us more lies and try to explain these away. I agree to his challenge that if Jesus rose from the dead, Christianity is true and Islam is false, since the Qur'an teaches that Jesus did not die on the cross. But in order to win this debate, I do not have to show that the resurrection of Jesus did not occur. I only have to show that the argument Paul is providing us does not work. Here's why. Let us suppose that Paul was also telling us that purple polka-dotted geese on Pluto are responsible for all of the unexplained phenomena in the universe. It would be his responsibility to give us evidence that his position is true. It would not be my responsibility to show that these alien fowl do not exist. If he told us that his proof for them is a dream he had of these birds when he was a little child, that would be very weak evidence and we would not be obligated to embrace his position. In fact, we would be irrational to do so.

The same is true of Jesus's resurrection. I do not believe it, but I say to Paul, "If you want me to believe it, provide good evidence and I will believe." But he has not. And so I am a Muslim, because I know what I saw and I know the Qur'an is Allah's word. Even if I did not provide any proof for the Qur'an, Christianity still loses if Jesus did not rise from the dead.

I'll continue to expound on why Paul's first fact, that Jesus died on the cross, is unacceptable. Paul did not address many of my objections to his reasons we can know that Jesus really died. For example, he did not say anything regarding Pilate's being amazed that Jesus had already died when Joseph requested his body. Neither did he say anything regarding the centurion's confession that Jesus was the Son of God. This shows that the centurion was a follower of Jesus, and a disciple would not kill his master. Rather, he would try to think of a way to free him.

Paul attempted to show us that the spear would have ensured Jesus was dead. What he neglected to mention is that the Greek word for stabbing used by John really only means to prod, as though trying to wake a person.[4] There is no reason to think a small prodding would kill anyone.

So we see good reasons to doubt Paul's assertion that Jesus died while on the cross. That was Paul's first fact. I will now proceed to his second fact: the empty tomb. I said that Paul never mentioned an empty tomb in his letters. He answered that in the term *resurrection*, an empty tomb is clearly implied, since resurrection refers to a bodily event. But I think Paul is trying to get out of a corner. Many scholars today hold that when Paul wrote about *resurrection* in his letters, he used it in a metaphorical sense to mean that Jesus now lives through his body, which is the church. Paul, you referred to the church on several occasions as the body of Christ.[5] This seems to be consistent with other statements you made on the matter. For example, in your famous chapter on resurrection bodies, you said that our current body is sown *natural* and raised *spiritual*.[6] There it is from your own writings! The New Revised Standard Version makes it as clear as water from a mountain spring: "It is sown a physical body, it is raised a spiritual body."[7] According to you, we are buried in a physical body and raised in a spiritual or immaterial body. So, Paul, you tried to deceive us again this evening. But you did not succeed.

Paul made another big mistake. I suggested the possibility that the disciples had gone to the wrong tomb and discovered it empty, concluding Jesus had risen. He answered that the Jewish and Roman authorities would have merely checked the correct tomb for the body if this was the case. But how can he be so certain of that? If the New Testament is accurate, Jesus's resurrection was not first proclaimed publicly until about fifty days after his resurrection.[8] This creates two further challenges. First, after fifty days Jesus's corpse would have decayed to the point of being unrecognizable; and second, Paul's answer assumes that the location of the body was known.

Remember that I had cited the Christian scholar John Dominic Crossan, who believes the empty tomb tradition is a legend. He holds that Jesus's body, or his substitute, as many Muslims believe, was left on the cross after he had died. The corpse was eaten by scavengers, then later discarded in a common pit. Accordingly, since Christians may not have known the location of Jesus's corpse, they invented the story of the empty tomb much later in order to explain the lack of knowledge of its location. After scavengers and decomposition, could anyone have identified the corpse? The resurrection of Jesus would have been an easy story to tell. Others would believe it. It could not be disproved. So this answer by Paul to refute the wrong-tomb theory is completely unsatisfactory. Therefore, contrary to the unfounded assertions of Paul, we have absolutely no reason to hold that Jesus had a tomb, much less that it was empty.

Lastly, we will again consider Paul's third fact: the appearances. I refuted the testimonies he provided from Clement and himself that the disciples were saying Jesus had been raised. Even if Clement knew Peter, he is still writing sixty-five years after Jesus. Memories become corrupted over that amount of time. So the accuracy of Clement's report is dubious. Paul then denied inventing Christianity as it is now known and said that the view that he did has been abandoned by nearly all scholars since the late 1970s. But these are Christian scholars. Furthermore, as I stated earlier, I am not interested in what a majority of scholars say, since what is accepted today is many times denied tomorrow. For example, not long ago scholars said the view that *Jesus* started Christianity as we know it had been largely abandoned because they believed *Paul* invented it. Which group of scholars are we to believe? That is why as a Muslim I base my doctrines, my beliefs, and my life on the Qur'an, which does not change. It is the word of Allah, the most merciful and compassionate.

Paul said that I attacked the accuracy of the Gospels because I am afraid to confront the facts he provided. I am not afraid to confront the facts you have given us, Paul. If you do not think I confronted them before, I have confronted them now and destroyed them.

In conclusion, we have seen that all of Paul's arguments against the Qur'an have failed. The Qur'an remains standing strong as the word of Allah, totally accurate. His attacks were like throwing bread against a stone fortress. They are useless. We have also seen that the three facts he uses to support his position that Jesus was resurrected are not facts at all.

Muhammad turns and walks away. Leaving no time for silence, a lone voice yells in Arabic, "Allahu Akbar!" which means "Allah is great!" And as expected, the Muslim attendees stand up in near unison and in one voice yell, "Allahu Akbar! Allahu Akbar! Allahu Akbar!" While the chant continues, two men from the stadium staff come up on the stage, pick up the podium, and move it to the back of the stage. Two more men bring a coffee table onto the stage and place it in front of the three men who remain seated. While this is occurring, Dr. Bahkr asks Dr. Sweeney, "Who do you think is winning?"

Although Sweeney does not consider herself to be a Christian, she is more drawn to Paul's historical approach to truth. But she does not want to offend Bahkr, who she is certain believes Muhammad to be ahead at the moment, so she says, "I think it's close."

She begins to ponder the value of truth in matters of religion. Until that moment she has seen little value in thinking of religious matters in terms of truth. After all, she sees no way of testing religious truth. But has she been wrong? Has Paul provided a means for verifying a particular worldview? Prior to this debate, she had not given much thought to the question of whether God exists, much less whether he has re-

vealed himself through a particular religion. She had thought that if God truly exists, he, she, or it does not care what one believes, only that one lives a moral life. But now, as she listens to the debate, she realizes that if what Paul is saying is true and Jesus has actually risen from the dead, the truth of Christianity will be confirmed, and that will present her with something she will have to think about very seriously. A shift in her worldview will be required.

Her thoughts will have to be placed on hold, however. The moderator, Bowers, is quieting the crowd and beginning to speak.

6

Discussion Period: Part One

Moderator: We have come to the discussion period of tonight's debate. You've heard a lot of arguments from Paul and Muhammad. At this point in a debate, when both representatives are highly informed and persuasive in their own right, the debate can appear to be at a tie. That's why the period that we are about to enter into is so vital. It allows both representatives to spend more time addressing crucial points. So consider what has occurred so far to be the laying of a foundation, building up to this part, where the issues will be scrutinized more carefully. Here's how this period works. I'm going to play a more active role as moderator and ask questions of Paul and Muhammad. Although I respect both of these men, I am not going to go easy on either of them. Our goal is to get to the truth, wherever that may lead us. Muhammad and Paul are free to interject their thoughts anytime they desire.

So let's begin. Paul, I would like to address the first question to you. You are aware that over the past one hundred years a lot has been said that calls your credibility into question. Muhammad accused you of inventing Christianity as we know it today. He claims that the Christianity that presents Jesus as more than a prophet, as the Son of God and even God, is not the Christianity that Jesus taught. Now, I only partially agree with you when you say that the majority of today's scholars have rejected the view that you invented Christianity. That does not fully address Muhammad's objection. Even if it is true that you did not invent Christianity—and we are all waiting to hear your reasons why we should not believe that you did—this does not eliminate the possibility that you taught some things about Jesus of which he would not have approved. So my question to you, Paul, has two parts: why shouldn't we hold that you invented Christianity, and if you did not invent it, how can we be confident that you did not push a higher view of Jesus than he would approve of?

Paul: Well, that is a great question, and I thank you for asking it. Let me start by addressing the first part of your question, which concerns Muhammad's accusation that I invented Christianity as it is known today. I was surprised when some theologians began to suggest this in the latter half of the 1800s, because the theory has so many problems.

Clement of Rome and Polycarp were disciples of the apostles.[1] Clement was apparently trained by Peter and Polycarp by John. Peter and John were two of the three disciples closest to Jesus and became prominent leaders of the church in the first century. So having writings by their disciples is very helpful.[2] Answer this question for yourself: if I had practically invented the major doctrines to which Muhammad referred—that Jesus is the Son of God and even God—since Clement and Polycarp were so close to Peter and John, wouldn't we expect them to rebuke me for deviating in my teachings from what their mentors had taught? Not only are such rebukes absent but Clement and Polycarp spoke very highly of me in their writings. Clement mentions the persecution and death of the "greatest and most righteous pillars" of the church. He then names Peter and me as examples.[3] Polycarp wrote that I "accurately and reliably taught the word concerning the truth."[4] Again, I ask you: if my teachings deviated from the teachings of the other apostles, why would their disciples refer to me as one of the church's "greatest and most righteous pillars" and write that I "accurately and reliably taught the word"? Why not instead rebuke me or say that people should not believe as Paul teaches but rather remember what the original disciples had taught as they had learned from their Lord, Jesus?

Another thing for you to consider is that if I was responsible for inventing Christianity, wouldn't it be likely that my writings would be favored over the other New Testament works by the early church leaders who wrote during the first six hundred years of Christianity? More than eighteen thousand pages of their writings have survived. When you look through these writings, you find that they quoted from and alluded to the Gospels many more times than they quoted from and alluded to my writings. These "memoirs" of the apostles, as Justin referred to them in AD 150, were appealed to much more than my writings.[5]

Muhammad: That is irrelevant, Paul. The Gospels were written after your writings. They weren't written by the traditional authors, either. So for all we know, they incorporated some of what the disciples had taught and some of what you taught that reflects a higher view of Jesus, on whom be peace.

Paul: The first point I made regarding Clement and Polycarp is relevant. And so is the second concerning the Gospels. That the Gospels were written after my letters is irrelevant if they come from sources independent of my letters and are at least based in the tradition that had been passed down by the disciples. And we know that they were, since most of what they contain is not found in my letters and is in line with the *kerygma*. My letters are instructions to the churches, whereas the Gospels are biographies of Jesus. I'm never even mentioned in them.

Muhammad: Let's talk about the *kerygma* for a moment.

Paul: I'd be glad to. But before we move on to that, I'd like to make two other points regarding the Gospels while we're discussing them. First, you cannot simply state as fact that the Gospels were not written by their traditional authors, Matthew, Mark, Luke, and John. There are still good reasons to believe that these traditional authors were the true authors.[6] Second, as I said earlier, all discussion of the Gospels is moot, since all of the data for Jesus's resurrection that I presented comes decades before the Gospels. So even if all of the Gospels had every one of the problems you have proposed, that would do nothing to undermine my argument for Jesus's resurrection, since the Gospels are later than the evidence I provided.

Muhammad: But legend, bias, and contradictions in them demonstrate that we cannot trust the accounts in them regarding Jesus's resurrection.

Paul: I don't agree with you at all, Muhammad. But I'll tell you this: for the sake of focusing on the evidence I provided, I'll grant you that the Gospels contain legend, bias, and contradictions as you claim and that they were not penned by their traditional authors. I don't believe this. But for the sake of our debate, I'll grant it to you. Now, let's put this in perspective. We have unreliable Gospels. Does this mean that the sources I provided that are decades earlier are unreliable simply because the Gospels are unreliable? Muslims today know that legend can be found in the early writings called the *hadith*. Does that mean there is legend in the Qur'an, which is earlier? Moreover, Muslims are well aware that much legend exists in the *hadith*. So would you have us believe that none of the *hadith* are trustworthy? That is why this entire argument concerning the Gospels does not work. You're attacking a hill on which my army doesn't stand.

Muhammad: I'll come back to the Gospels later, since I believe problems with them are relevant. But let's go back to the *kerygma*. You gave the creed in your first letter to the Corinthian church as an example of *kerygma*. But as I pointed out, this is found in *your* letter. You could have written that creed yourself.

Paul: I could say that you wrote the Qur'an. But you would give reasons why we shouldn't believe that. Then it would be up to everyone listening to determine if those reasons were good enough to overcome my assertion. Thus, we will do the same here. I provided that creed because it is a great example of *kerygma*. First, when introducing the creed, I told the Corinthians that when I had been with them a few years earlier,[7] I delivered to them what I had likewise received. The terms "delivered" and "received" were common terms denoting the imparting of oral tradition. I said that I had received this tradition from others. Second, since oral tradition was spoken, we might expect to find traces of its original language, which would have probably been Aramaic, the primary Jewish dialect of the day. And we do find a few of these traces, such as the threefold use of the phrase "and that" which introduces every clause. Listen to the passage:

That Christ died for our sins according to the Scriptures
and that he was buried
and that he was raised on the third day according to the
    Scriptures
and that he appeared to Cephas.[8]

And *Cephas* is the Aramaic word for *Peter*. Third, look at the parallelism that exists. Long, short, long, short. The first and third clauses are long, whereas the second and fourth are short. Fourth and finally, a few terms are in the creed that I never use throughout my letters.[9] In fact, I used different terms elsewhere to say the same things. This should indicate to you that I didn't author this creed. Besides, after quoting the creed in verses 3 through 7, I refer to this in verses 11, 12, and 14 as *kerygma*, the official and formal teaching of the disciples.

Muhammad: All you have just shared with us proves that it is a creed. But you could have been lying to the Corinthians then and to us now by saying you had received this creed from others. How do we know this is not what you are doing?

Paul: That's a fair question. Remember that there are terms that I do not use elsewhere. Scholars refer to these as "non-Pauline terms." This favors someone else authoring the creed. Consider also that the Corinthian Christians knew what the other apostles were teaching and thus would know if I was teaching something different than the other apostles were teaching. In fact, some had formed groups that went beyond being merely fan clubs of these church leaders. In 1 Corinthians 1:11–12, I wrote:

> For it was made clear to me concerning you, my brethren, by Chloe's people, that there are quarrels among you. And I say this, that each one of you is saying, "I am of Paul," and "I of Apollos," and "I of Cephas," and "I of Christ."

Obviously, they must have heard Apollos, Peter, Jesus, and me or knew what we were teaching in order to say these things. So they had teachings from other apostles to which they could compare mine.

Muhammad: But look at the point you were making to the Corinthians. You said they were quarrelling over who they were following! You all must have been teaching different doctrines for them to say this.

Paul: Not at all. I admit that James and I, for example, didn't always see eye to eye on everything. He leaned toward a more rigid lifestyle than I did. But that's related more to personal preferences than to theology. For example, if he were alive today, he probably wouldn't have a television in his home, whereas I would have one in order to keep current on events to help me communicate with others. Now remember, Luke reports in Acts that when some questions arose regarding Gentiles in the church and whether they needed to be circumcised and follow the Jewish law, this was all discussed in the Jerusalem church where James presided. Everyone agreed that Gentiles were welcome in the church and that my ministry would be primarily to them. They even commended Barnabas and me to the church, as Luke reported.[10] I reported this as well when I wrote to the Galatian church.[11] The quarrels I wrote about in 1 Corinthians 1:11–12 were not over major doctrines. They were related more to style, preference, and personalities. They were not of the magnitude of the quarrel that occurred after your death, Muhammad, related to who your successor would be—Abu Bakr or your cousin Ali.

So we see that the passage we are considering in 1 Corinthians 15 has all the marks of being the official teaching of the apostles and that it did not originate with me.

Moderator: Paul, I struggle with something you said in your letter to the Romans, chapter 3, verses 7 and 8. You wrote:

But if by my lie the truth of God abounded to his glory, why am I still judged as a sinner? And why not say (as we are blasphemed and just as some claim that we say), "Let us do evil in order that good may come"?

It seems to me you are saying here that it is okay to lie if God's truth, specifically the Christian gospel, is preached. What do you say to this?

Paul: I ask you to read that statement in context. I have just finished saying in chapter 2 that a true Jew is one who has partaken in God's covenant through Jesus, not one who was simply born a Jew. I begin chapter 3 as a dialogue with a Jew who is distorting Christian doctrine with faulty reasoning. He starts by asking, "If Christianity is true as you claim, is there any advantage that remains to being one who is born a Jew?" "Most certainly," I answer, "because it was the Jews who had been entrusted with God's oracles." But then the Jew replies, "If some Jews did not believe, won't this nullify God's faithfulness?" And I answer, "No way! God is true, even if every man is a liar!" Then the Jew replies, "But if our rebellion as Jews results in God demonstrating his power through punishment of our unbelief, then our evil produces good, and how can a righteous God award his wrath when our unbelief results in good?" This is crazy reasoning, isn't it? But this is a sample of the ways in which we early Jewish Christians were misunderstood. So I answer, "No way! Otherwise, how will God judge the world?"

The Jew comes back with two final objections: "If I lie and I'm punished, that punishment promotes the glory of God. So, Paul, what your theology suggests is that we should do evil that good may result." This is where you misunderstood my letter. You thought *I* was the one suggesting that lying is good when it was the Jew with whom I was dialoguing. Notice that in verse 8 I also say that we, the Christian apostles, are *slandered* as saying, "Let us do evil that good may come." We never said, "Let us do evil that good may come." We were falsely reported by certain Jews as saying this. That is why I follow immediately with the statement concerning them, "They deserve their condemnation."

To sum this up, some Jews were attempting to trap me. I tried to show this is bad reasoning on their part, but then they said it was the logical outcome of *my* reasoning, since they thought that I supported lying in order to bring about good. But I don't. Do you understand? The statement that we should do evil that good may come is what they said all of us apostles were saying. But we were not.

Moderator: In the fourth century, Eusebius made an interesting statement. In his writing titled *Evangelical Preparation*, he writes, "That it will be necessary sometimes to use falsehood as a remedy for the benefit of those who require such a mode of treatment."[12] It seems here that we certainly have a Christian promoting deceit in order to advance Christianity. And Eusebius is considered to be a great church historian!

Paul: Once again, you have misunderstood what was written. You have to consider the context. This statement by Eusebius appears in the table of contents of his book. It is a section heading. There is interesting content in his main text. His thesis is that great philosophers borrowed from the Hebrew Scriptures. As an example he goes to the writings of Plato. In *Laws*, Plato is having a dialogue just as I had in the Romans passage we just discussed.[13] Plato is having a discussion concerning societal laws. He says that it should be taught that the righteous person will ultimately have a happier life than the wicked person, even though the wicked may have power and possessions. Plato says he believes this is true, but even if it turns out not to be, teaching it is still good, since people will tend to live more righteously if they believe this. (He actually uses the term "good lie,"[14] and one major translator renders it "useful fiction"[15] because ill will is absent.)

Eusebius uses this passage to support his belief that others copied thoughts from the Hebrew Scriptures. He compares Plato's words with the Old Testament, saying, "Now you may find in the Hebrew Scriptures also thousands of such passages concerning God as though He were jealous, or sleeping, or angry, or subject to any other human passions, which passages are adopted for the benefit of those who need this mode of instruction." Eusebius is saying that passages which present God as jealous, sleeping, or angry describe him that way in order to aid us in understanding his actions. They could be figures of speech[16] or they could be literally true. But even if God does not experience these things, the descriptions themselves are "useful fiction."

The Hebrew and Christian Scriptures never endorse lying or encourage one to lie. In fact, truth telling is strongly taught.[17] So even if I'm wrong in my interpretation of Eusebius, it does not matter. The Christian Scriptures clearly teach that lying is wrong. I encourage you to also read Eusebius's sequel to *Evangelical Preparation* called *Evangelical Demonstration*. In book 3, chapter 5, he makes a statement about lying in order to bring people into the kingdom of Christ. However, in context you see that he is obviously writing sarcastically. He clearly intends for his readers to understand that doing so is preposterous. Since he teaches against lying in the sequel to *Evangelical Preparation*, no interpretation of the passage you mentioned would seem to merit the conclusion that Eusebius encouraged people to lie in order to bring others into the kingdom.

So I hope we can lay to rest this crazy thought that Christians, including me, think it is okay to lie to others to accomplish good. Christians do not believe this, as is clear throughout our Scriptures.

7

Discussion Period: Part Two

Moderator: Muhammad, I have a question I'd like to ask you. I find the Muslim view of what happened to Jesus to be very fascinating. God certainly has the power to substitute someone for Jesus by making that person identical to him in appearance. He certainly has the power to make Jesus appear to have died on the cross, fooling others who removed him and buried him. However, I think Paul raised a good point when he said that if no good reasons exist for trusting the Qur'an on this matter, the historian must conclude that Jesus was crucified and died as a result.

Paul questioned you on the Qur'an by arguing that the founder of Mormonism, Joseph Smith, claimed that an angel appeared to him too. Paul asked why we should believe your testimony while rejecting Smith's. You replied that Smith could have seen evil jinn who deceived him. Well, okay, that's possible. But what about Paul's second challenge to the Qur'an? He challenged the test presented in it for knowing if it is from Allah. He claimed that it fails its own test when sura 1 is compared with Psalm 19. To that you replied that Paul is a blasphemer and you don't care what he thinks. I don't find that sufficient. What if Paul had merely replied that he didn't care what I thought when I challenged him on what he wrote in Romans? So I would like to hear you say more on this matter.

Muhammad: Muslims never claim that translations of the Qur'an are sufficient. In order to appreciate the Qur'an fully, one must read it in Arabic. Paul, do you read Arabic?

Paul: No. Just Hebrew, Aramaic, Greek, and Latin. Well, I also recently learned English for this debate, as did you!

Muhammad: Unless you can read Arabic, you cannot make such a comparison. The Qur'an has a beauty when it is read in Arabic, a certain rhythm and sound that cannot be reproduced when attempting to write a passage on Allah. Thus your comparison of sura 1 with Psalm 19 is insufficient.

Paul: Do you read Hebrew?

Muhammad: No.

Paul: Then how can you make such a claim? The Psalms are a collection of songs which when sung in Hebrew have a beautiful rhythm and sound. In my opinion, the Hebrew language has a much nicer sound to it than Arabic. Plus, as I noted, Psalm 19 is much fuller in meaning than the first sura.

Muhammad: I did not create the test. You speak as though I wrote the Qur'an. I did not write it. I could not read or write then. Allah is the author of the Qur'an, and he is the one who made the test. I believe Allah. Since you do not speak or read Arabic, you are not in a position to make the judgment that Psalm 19 is superior to sura 1.

Paul: I have a problem believing that the all-powerful God would give a test that only Arabic-reading people can take. How many of today's Muslims can read Arabic? Twenty percent? This is another reason why I do not believe it is a good test.

Moderator: I don't think we're getting very far on this topic. Let's change course. Paul, I have a question for you that concerns the death of Jesus. Muhammad is correct that if we cannot be certain that Jesus in fact died, we have no way to hold with certainty that he rose from the dead. If God rescued Jesus by providing a substitute or healed him in the tomb after he was mistaken for dead, it makes sense that if Jesus appeared to his disciples afterward and they thought he had died, they would have thought he had resurrected. As I see it, both you and Muhammad hold that the Jewish leadership came to arrest Jesus, they crucified someone who they thought was Jesus, and afterward, Jesus appeared alive to a number of his disciples. Where you differ is that you believe God resurrected Jesus, whereas Muhammad believes God rescued him. Are we just splitting hairs here?

Paul: Not when you consider what is at stake. If what happened to Jesus was a resurrection, then he died, since resurrection means raising from the dead. Jesus's atoning death for mankind is a fundamental doctrine of Christianity. If it did not occur and Jesus was rescued, as the Qur'an states, Christianity is false. On the other hand, if Jesus was resurrected, his atoning death looks much more likely. Moreover, if Jesus died, the Qur'an is wrong on the subject of what happened to Jesus. In this case, Islam is false given its view that the Qur'an is either without error in its entirety or it is not the word of Allah. The interpretation of what happened to Jesus could not be more important. So it appears that the ultimate issue for us to discuss for the remainder of the evening is whether we should believe Jesus died.

Moderator: That leads us to consider some outstanding issues regarding Jesus's death. You argued, Paul, that since Jesus had predicted his violent death, if he did not die violently or actually die at all, that would make him a false prophet, a view unacceptable to Muslims. Muhammad provided two answers. First, he said that a prophet does not need to be 100 percent accurate on everything he thinks or says when not claiming to speak the counsel of God. His second answer was that Jesus did not predict his violent death when he talked about the sign of Jonah. I want to discuss both of these with you. But let's focus on his first answer for the time being. Do you think that a true prophet of God must have all of his facts straight on everything all of the time?

Paul: No. I agree with Muhammad on this point. But I do think that true prophets need to be right on major issues on which they claim to speak for God. And the physical death of Jesus is a major issue in Christianity. Let's consider a major issue for the Muslim faith: the origin of the Qur'an. Muhammad, when the angel Gabriel began appearing to you and giving you revelations, did you immediately conclude that he was from Allah?

Muhammad: Not at all. I knew that Satan may have been behind it and that I may have been possessed by demons. In fact, this was what I first suspected.[1] I did not jump to the conclusion that the angel came from Allah.

Paul: Very well. But what if you were wrong in your judgment and the personage was in fact from Satan as you first suspected? Your judgment that the angel came from Allah was not necessarily made in your capacity as a prophet. That would be to argue in a circle: I know the angel is from Allah because I am a prophet, and I know I am a prophet because the angel told me so. This is like a hamster on a wheel. Why is the hamster crawling? Because the wheel moves. Why does the wheel move? Because the hamster is crawling. With this type of argument, like the hamster, you get nowhere.

[At this comment there is an outburst of laughter from the crowd. Then Paul continues.]

What if you were wrong? I think that in suggesting Jesus could have been mistaken on such a major issue as his violent death, you have opened the door for considering that the origin of the Qur'an was not from Allah but was demonic, as you originally suspected. Thus what you suggest does not weaken the Christian position, since you can provide no evidence that Jesus was mistaken in predicting his violent death. However, you have shaken the foundations of Islam as a result of your willingness to open the door to the possibility that a prophet can be wrong on major issues.

Muhammad: What you are saying hinges on the predictions of Jesus, on whom be peace, that he would die a violent death. And I clearly demonstrated that he did not make those predictions and that Matthew actually presents Jesus, peace be upon him, as a false prophet, since he did not fulfill the sign of Jonah.

Paul: You are mistaken concerning the sign of Jonah. The sign of Jonah was an analogy Jesus provided concerning his death. Analogies rarely if ever match on every point, and this one doesn't. Otherwise, Jesus would have been in the earth because he was being disobedient to God's will rather than because he obeyed. And Jesus would have had to meet his fate at sea rather than on a cross.

Muhammad: I agree. However, we must note what points are presented as analogous by Jesus, peace be upon him. He says "just as Jonah was three days and three nights in the belly of the great fish, so will the Son of Man be three days and three nights in the heart of the earth."[2] The great fish is not analogous. But the three days and three nights are. And that is where the problem arises. If the Gospels are accurate, Jesus was only in the tomb for one day and two nights.

Paul: That's right. But you have failed to recognize that the phrase "three days and three nights" is a Jewish idiom meaning a short period of time and does not necessarily have to include three days and three nights.[3] Today we might speak of a long task taking "forever." We mean that it will take a long time. We do not mean that it will take an infinite amount of time and is incapable of being completed. Likewise, someone may say that something will take "only a minute." This means a very short time, not sixty seconds. These are simply English idioms. Idioms exist in all languages. In the book of Esther, Esther tells her fellow Jews the following:

> Go, assemble all the Jews who are found in Susa, and fast for me; do not eat or drink for *three days, night or day. I and my maidens also will fast in the same way.* And thus I will go in to the king, which is not according to the law; and if I perish, I perish.[4]

Now, notice what happens two verses later:

> Now it came about *on the third day*[5] that Esther put on her royal robes and stood in the inner court of the king's palace in front of the king's rooms, and the king was sitting on his royal throne in the throne room, opposite the entrance to the palace.[6]

Esther did not wait a full three days and three nights. She went to the king on the third day. So that would be two days plus a number of hours. Let's look at one other passage. Matthew 27:63–64 reports that after Jesus's crucifixion, the Jewish leaders approached Pilate and said:

> Sir, we remember that while living that deceiver said, "After three days I will rise." Therefore, order the grave to be secured until the third day, lest his disciples come and steal him away and say to the people, "He was raised from the dead," and the last deceit will be worse than the first.

Matthew, the same author who reported the "three days and three nights" in the sign of Jonah, is later reporting the request of the Jewish leaders. Notice that they say that Jesus predicted he would rise *after* three days. So what do they do? They request that the grave be secured by guards *until* the third day. If the term "after three days" is a Jewish idiom that does not mean a full seventy-two hours, this passage has no conflict. But if by it Jesus meant he would be dead *at least* seventy-two hours before rising, then the Jewish leaders are foolish to request that the grave be secured "until the third day." In other words, they intend to pull the guard just before Jesus said he would rise, which would leave nearly twenty-four hours for the disciples to steal his body. You see? Understanding "three days" in a literal sense does not make sense. Therefore, when we consider two Jewish writings, one from the Old Testament and one from the New Testament, the terms "after three days" and "three days and three nights" seem to be a Jewish idiom that is not in conflict with the earliest Christian claims that Jesus was raised "on the third day."

Moderator: I'll agree that what you're saying is a possibility. But it is also possible that three days and three nights could mean that precise amount of time. Otherwise, how else would someone indicate that three days and three nights is the precise timing meant? So we are going to have to look at probabilities. In other words, which interpretation seems most likely in reference to the sign of Jonah?

Paul: Yes. I agree. We should note that the sign of Jonah is only one of many reports of Jesus predicting his death. I think everyone agrees that a sound hermeneutic interprets questionable passages in light of clear ones. We do not interpret one questionable passage contrary to the many clear ones. So let's look briefly at some of these other reports. Matthew, the same author who reports the sign of

Jonah prediction, has Jesus predicting his death at least four other times, all of which say "on the third day" and "in three days."[7] Matthew did not have a problem with it, and he understood the language better than all of you. This is just like the Esther passage where "three days, night or day" and "on the third day" are not in conflict. Moreover, clear predictions are found five times in the earliest Gospel, which is Mark.[8] Four of the five are multiply attested in Matthew and Luke. The fifth is multiply-attested in Matthew.

The predictions also appear in multiple forms, indicating the probability that they are independent traditions and that their origin was before the writing of Mark. For example, Jesus gives a straight prediction that he will die a violent death in Mark 10:33–34 and also makes this prediction through a parable in Mark 12:7–8. Even the highly skeptical scholars of the Jesus Seminar hold we can have a high degree of confidence that Jesus actually predicted his violent death.[9]

Moderator: Hmmm. I can understand how the phrases "on the third day" and "three days and three nights" can mean virtually the same. But I'm still struggling with the three days part. All the predictions mention the number three. Even the creed in 1 Corinthians 15 says "he was raised on the third day." Yet, if we are to believe the Gospels, we are still only looking at one and a half days, since Jesus was buried at around six o'clock Friday evening and raised before six o'clock Sunday morning.

Paul: That's a fair question. Let me make a few points. First, I already stated that the term "three days" can refer to a short period of time, just like in some contexts "forever" can refer to days or even hours. Second, the authors of the Gospels apparently saw no problems between the two. They all report Jesus's predictions concerning his resurrection on the third day and then report that it occurred in about one and a half days.

Third, it could be that any part of a day referred to a day. Let us suppose that two sports teams are going to play two games in your city. The first game is tonight, the second is tomorrow, and they'll leave town on the third day. They could be leaving in the morning. Or let us suppose that their final game will be on the morning of the third day and after three days they'll leave town. Even though they arrived at night on the first day and left early on the third day, we would still call it a three-day trip. I doubt you would see a tension with that. So why is there a problem when the same appears in reference to Jesus's resurrection? Finally, even if all of the possible solutions I have provided are wrong, it doesn't matter. The tensions regarding Jesus's predictions about his time in the tomb and the resurrection narratives all appear in the Gospels. So, again, for the sake of our debate, I could grant that all of these problems are real and unsolvable, and my argument would not be affected, since almost all of my evidence comes from outside the Gospels and for the most part is earlier. Problems with the Gospels do not do anything to show any problems with the other data that I cited. To be even more specific, we have just seen that Matthew did not present Jesus as a false prophet. However, even if he had, it would not matter, since he is not included in the sources I have appealed to this evening.

8

Discussion Period: Part Three

Moderator: A question for Muhammad. I want to stay on the subject of the death of Jesus a little longer until we have worked through the issues. This way our audience will have the opportunity to reflect on what has been said and make their own decision. Paul has argued that there is historical evidence that Jesus died on the cross: it's multiply attested, non-Christian sources reported it, it's unlikely that anyone would survive crucifixion, and medical opinions about what occurs during a crucifixion argue strongly against survival. Thus, in the absence of good evidence for his survival, historians must conclude that Jesus was indeed crucified and died as a result. You have argued that the evidence to the contrary is that the Qur'an states that Jesus did not die on the cross. Would you say that if the Qur'an did not exist, the evidence would be enough to conclude that Jesus in fact died by being crucified?

    Muhammad: Yes. Certainly, I agree with that. But that is like saying that apart from the eyewitness who saw what happened, an eyewitness who is known to always tell the truth, the circumstantial evidence would lead us to a different conclusion that would be wrong.

Moderator: Now, I know you can provide several examples where you believe the Qur'an makes accurate scientific statements that you could not have known when you received the revelation. I'm also aware that Paul could present several similar arguments for the truth of the Bible. So I'm fine with us not broaching that subject today and leaving that for another debate. I think it will take us too far off the subject of Jesus's resurrection. So, Muhammad, I appreciate the fact that you did not focus on these in your rebuttal.

Paul, let me come back to you for a moment. Muhammad pointed out how the earliest Gospel, Mark, notes Pilate's amazement when he learns that Jesus had died so soon. People were known to survive crucifixion for as long as a few days. However, Jesus, whom you believe is the Son of God, died within six hours of being placed on the cross. This does seem to support the Muslim suspicion that he may have been removed while alive. And you must admit that the Gospels report that Pilate did not want to kill Jesus. So maybe he found a way to let him be removed early. Can you explain that?

Paul: Well, again, you are talking about the Gospels. What do they have to do with the much earlier data I provided? With the exception of James's view of his half brother Jesus prior to his resurrection, I did not appeal to the Gospels a single time in my argument for Jesus's resurrection. I am not attempting to dodge the issue. I will answer it. I am merely pointing out that it does not matter in the scheme of things in this debate.

Muhammad: You are surely mistaken, Paul. It does matter. If the Gospels are truthful here, they may provide clues regarding what really happened to Jesus. It is important because you do not report these things in your writings.

Paul: That is correct. I do not report them because I was not writing a biography of Jesus. My letters concern issues in the various churches of my day. But what I say regarding my experience of Jesus and what the disciples were claiming about what happened to Jesus after his crucifixion are still very early and multiply-attested.

I would like to note, however, that your objections involving Pilate and the centurion's confession are a bit confusing to me. You have spent a lot of effort casting doubt on the reliability of the Gospels in this debate. You claimed that their authors were biased, that the real authors' identities are unknown, that they contradict one another, that there are contradictions even within the same Gospel, and that many of the stories were not meant to be understood literally. The conclusion asserted by Muhammad is that we cannot trust what the Gospels are saying.

Then you immediately appeal to reports in those same Gospels as evidence against Jesus's resurrection. In other words, you argue that the Gospels are unreliable, then appeal to reports in them as though they are accurate as evidence against Jesus's death and resurrection. This is "cafeteria criticism," where you take what looks good to your taste and leave what does not. It is historiographical hypocrisy. The death of Jesus is much more strongly attested than Pilate's amazement and the centurion's confession. So if you are going to reject Jesus's death, all the more you should reject reports by the same Gospels of Pilate's amazement and the centurion's confession. On the other hand, if you are going to accept the latter, then all the more you should accept the former.

With that said, let me speak specifically regarding Pilate's amazement and his desire to preserve Jesus's life. From a medical viewpoint, extreme scourging may have brought on hypovolemic shock[1] and expedited his death. That Jesus was unable to carry his cross all the way may indicate that his scourging was especially brutal. Another explanation is that from the standpoint of the Gospels, Jesus had no medical cause of death. He gave up his life willingly when he had atoned for the sins of the world. He said, "The reason my Father loves me is that I lay down my life—only to take it up again. No one takes it from me, but I lay it down of my own accord. I have authority to lay it down and authority to take it up again."[2] When we consider the strong possibility that Jesus had been treated more brutally than normal crucifixion victims and that if he was the divine Son of God he had the power to give up his human life when he saw fit, Pilate's amazement should be no more than our amusement.

Moreover, although Pilate may initially have had an interest in releasing Jesus, once Jesus was accused of being a threat to Caesar, Pilate would have abandoned any such interest out of a desire for self-preservation. Remember that in the midst of Jesus's trial the Jewish leaders had said, "If you release Jesus, you are not Caesar's friend; everyone who makes himself out to be a king opposes Caesar."[3]

It is helpful to note that Pilate had a Roman protector named Sejanus who was executed by the Emperor Tiberius in AD 31 for being suspected of plotting against him. If Jesus was crucified in AD 33 as many hold, Pilate would have been in a weak position, and Tiberius would have had a close eye on him. The last thing he would have wanted to do was anything that might have been perceived as protecting someone claiming to be a king against Caesar.

Muhammad: Then there's the centurion who said, "Truly this man was the Son of God!"[4] No one would make this statement unless he was a Christian, and wouldn't a Christian refuse to crucify his Lord? He would have done everything in his power to see that Jesus did not die on that cross!

Paul: We have no indication that the centurion was a Christian. Again, you cannot look at a single statement while ignoring the context in which it appears. Now notice the context. Mark reports that from around noon until three o'clock in the afternoon, darkness came over the whole land.[5] In the midst of this darkness in the middle of the day, Jesus yells, "My God! My God! Why have you forsaken me?" He said this in Aramaic. Some of the bystanders apparently did not understand Aramaic and thought he was calling for Elijah. Then Jesus uttered another loud cry and died. Mark reports that "when the centurion, who was there in front of him, saw the manner in which he breathed his last, he said, 'Truly, this man was the Son of God!'" Why did he make this confession? Because something had impressed him in the way Jesus had died! In other words, rather than casting doubt on Jesus's death, the centurion's confession actually points to it. Without being impressed with the manner *in which Jesus died*, the centurion would have made no confession. So I think the centurion's confession may also be called the centurion's conversion.

Muhammad: That is Mark's account. Matthew adds details that are very interesting. When Jesus died, Matthew reports:

> The veil of the temple was torn in two from top to bottom; and the earth shook and the rocks were split. The tombs were opened, and many bodies of the saints who had fallen asleep were raised; and coming out of the tombs after his resurrection they entered the holy city and appeared to many.[6]

If this really occurred, why is it, Paul, that Matthew is the only one who reported it? Such a big event should have been mentioned by many first-century authors! Matthew seems to have added some details to Mark's account or the story that was going around. So Jesus's death on the cross could have been more of the same.

Paul: So we seem to be in agreement that the centurion's statement is not a problem. Now, regarding Matthew's account of the phenomena that occurred at Jesus's death, I wouldn't be so quick to dismiss it as legend, since there are reasons to believe these things occurred.[7] But even if Matthew invented details as you suggest, that does not justify the conclusion that the story of Jesus's death had been invented too. Matthew may be using apocalyptic language—in other words, using grandiose word pictures in order to draw attention to the fact that he believes something special and big occurred at this moment in history. For example, Philo, a Jewish writer contemporary with Jesus and his apostles, believed eclipses were omens of the impending death of a king.[8] Plutarch,[9] Ovid,[10] Cicero,[11] Virgil,[12] and Josephus[13] all report that an eclipse occurred when Julius Caesar died. In Acts 2:20, Peter quotes from Joel 2:28–32,[14] where the sun turns to darkness and the moon to blood, and indicates this has been fulfilled in their presence. Cassius Dio reports that at the fall of Alexandria to the Romans, "the ghosts of the dead appeared."[15]

Matthew's report of opened tombs and their dead walking in Jerusalem may have a parallel in Ezekiel 37:12–13, where it is written:

> I will open your tombs, and I will bring you up out of your tombs, and I will lead you into the land of Israel.

Compare this with our passage in Matthew:

> The tombs were opened, and many bodies of the saints who had fallen asleep were raised; coming out of the tombs after his resurrection they entered the holy city and appeared to many.

So this passage is only a problem if you are unfamiliar with what Matthew may have been doing. If he is using apocalyptic language in his descriptions of what occurred at Jesus's death, he is doing so because he wants to emphasize that something huge occurred here. It is an exclamation point in the text exclaiming that a great king has died!

Muhammad: In that case, that creates another question that begs to be asked: if apocalyptic language is used here when the text speaks of tombs being opened and the dead being raised and appearing, wouldn't it be more consistent to interpret Jesus's resurrection in a similar manner? Could it be that when the Gospel writers said Jesus's tomb was empty, that he had risen from the dead, and that he had appeared in Jerusalem, this was apocalyptic language, a metaphor for saying that although Jesus is gone his teachings, power, and presence are still available through the church, which you yourself, Paul, called the "body of Christ"?

Paul: Maybe something I wrote before Matthew penned his Gospel would be helpful. In 1 Corinthians 15, I present an argument regarding the afterlife that depends on Jesus's resurrection being a historical fact. If it did not occur, my argument makes no sense whatsoever. So a literal bodily resurrection of Jesus is what I meant when I wrote about Jesus's resurrection, and that was prior to Matthew's Gospel being written. Moreover, an apocalyptic interpretation of Jesus's resurrection is hardly convincing as reason for the dramatic reversal of the hostile opinions of James and me toward the church. We were certainly knowledgeable of apocalyptic language. We would not convert based on a story we would have known to be fictitious.

Here is something else for your consideration. Remember that apocalyptic language is an exclamation point in the text that grabs the attention of the reader and says, "Hey! Look at this! Something big happened here!" When we read Matthew's report of the earthquake, the darkness on the earth, and the opening of tombs, his language is saying, "Hey! Look at this page! Hear what it is saying! A great king has died!" However, when we come to the Gospel accounts of Jesus's resurrection, it is very different. If it's apocalyptic language and Matthew is saying, "Hey! Look at this page! Hear what it is saying!" then we should see an even more important point or event to which the talk of a resurrection points. However, when we look at the page for that point or event, it is blank. Apocalyptic language points to something. But Jesus's resurrection never points to anything else. Instead, it is the event to which everything else points!

Muhammad: Unless it is pointing to the continuing power and presence of Jesus, on whom be peace, in the church. Then the apocalyptic language Matthew uses makes perfect sense without having to strain things by requiring Jesus's resurrection from the dead in a bodily sense.

Moderator: I think Muhammad may have touched on something very interesting and important. And I want to discuss it more thoroughly. But I think that will be more appropriate later as we discuss the empty tomb and the appearances. Certainly, Paul, you're going to have to address this issue at that time, because I think it is potentially devastating to your position that Jesus's literal resurrection from the dead is a real event in history. So let's put a bookmark here so that we can return later, and let me pull us back to the issue of Jesus's death for a moment. Paul, what about the Greek word John uses for piercing with the spear, that means to prod as if waking someone?[16]

Paul: I never used that passage as my evidence that Jesus died. So that's not the hill I'm on today. We are not debating the inspiration and inerrancy of the New Testament. That is a different debate, and it is not relevant to the evidence I have provided.

Moderator: But it is relevant. I agree with you that the accuracy of the New Testament is not the topic for debate this evening. But then, Paul, you proceed by quoting and appealing to much that is in the New Testament as though it is accurate. This is very similar to what you charged Muhammad with doing just a few moments ago. He rejects the accuracy of the New Testament, then appeals to it. On the other hand, you say the accuracy of the New Testament is not relevant to this debate, and then you appeal to it. It seems to me that the accuracy of the New Testament is a crucial issue in this debate.

Paul: Let me clarify my approach. Just like the Qur'an, the New Testament contains many things that we as historians simply cannot verify. So my approach is to present only data pertaining to Jesus's resurrection that can be verified. Regarding accuracy, Tacitus is considered to be the greatest Roman historian. Historians have found bias and errors throughout his writings. Does that mean that we cannot trust anything Tacitus wrote? What about events that were reported by another Roman historian, such as the great fire of Rome that occurred in AD 64? The accounts of that fire are found in the writings of a number of Roman historians who contradict one another on the extent of the fire as well as other details. Does this mean we should not believe that the fire itself occurred?[17] Of course not. If you rejected sources simply on the basis of inaccuracies, bias, and all the other challenges that have been raised against the Gospels, you would have to throw out so much that your knowledge of the past would go from libraries to pages. That's why challenges to the Gospels are irrelevant, and that's why I have limited my presentation and evidence strictly to what I can prove. I provided three historical facts and reasons why the majority of scholars regard these as facts.

Moderator: You mention the majority of scholars. Muhammad is absolutely correct in noting that scholars are many times wrong. He also said that you failed to mention that the majority of scholars do not hold that Jesus rose from the dead. So you appear to be selective in what you want to cite regarding the majority of scholars.

Paul: I agree with Muhammad that the majority of scholars have been wrong many times in the past and we can be certain they are wrong on some things they hold today. I never said or meant to suggest that we should believe something because the majority of scholars regard it as true. Instead, I presented three facts. I provided evidence and a number of reasons for holding these as facts. Then I added that the majority of scholars hold these as facts. Now, I am not suggesting by this that they are facts because the majority of scholars regard them as such. My purpose in mentioning the majority of scholars is to show that I am not alone in seeing the evidence I provided as convincing. I don't think that I have to apologize for having the majority of scholars on my side when it comes to my three facts. I think it is a weight on my side of the scale when, in addition to providing evidence, I can add that an impressive majority of scholars, including very skeptical ones who do not agree with my conclusion, find these data convincing. That is what I am trying to communicate. We may not agree on the conclusions. But we agree on the data. I don't blame Muhammad for not liking this approach, since he cannot use it when it comes to statements in the Qur'an regarding what happened to Jesus. Instead, he has to *believe completely contrary* to what the large majority of historians hold today.

Muhammad: That is totally misleading regarding the Qur'an. Many scientists, not just Muslim but also Western scientists, are amazed at the scientific statements in the Qur'an.

Paul: And do Muslims today cite these in Islamic literature?

Muhammad: Many times. Yes.[18]

Paul: And why is that? Why not simply assert that modern science has affirmed statements in the Qur'an?

Muhammad: Citing actual scientists who agree shows that this is not merely Islamic propaganda.

Paul: Precisely! And that is what I'm doing by citing historians. So you shouldn't object to it.

Moderator: Paul, you've mentioned the consensus of scholars a few times this evening. What's your source for this information?

Paul: Professor Gary Habermas is one of your scholars today. He recently spent several years compiling a bibliography of more than two thousand books and journal articles on Jesus's resurrection written between 1975 and 2005. Habermas catalogued where these scholars stand on more than one hundred issues pertaining to Jesus's resurrection. That's the source of my figures.[19]

9

Discussion Period: Part Four

Moderator: Let's bring this back on topic and go back to the spear and the meaning of piercing. Paul, what do you have to say regarding Muhammad's contention that John probably only meant that the soldier prodded Jesus with his spear as though to wake him?

Paul: I saw many crucifixions in my day and I can assure you that while on a cross, Jesus would not have been able to find a comfortable position in which he could fall asleep! I agree that the Greek word employed by John can mean "to prod." However, it can also mean "to stab" in such a way that you intended to kill. Josephus uses it in this manner in reference to the killing of a soldier.[1] And we have Quintilian, a Roman historian from the first century, saying that the executioner can bury the crucified dead once they have been pierced.[2] Thus I think it is clear that the best meaning to adopt for John's use of piercing Jesus after he had died on the cross is as Quintilian used it.

Moderator: Let me ask you one more question concerning crucifixion, Paul. Something remains troubling to me in relation to your view that Jesus died. Before I ask it, I want you to know that I am not trying to be unfair or biased against the Christian position in prying into these issues. The fact is that you presented the position that Jesus rose from the dead and thus you bear a greater burden of proof in this debate than Muhammad. If this was a debate titled "Is the Qur'an the Word of Allah?" then Muhammad would have a greater burden of proof than you. But that's not our topic. You have chosen to say that Jesus rose from the dead and thus Christianity is true and Islam is false. So you shoulder a heavier burden of proof to show that Jesus rose from the dead than Muhammad does to show that he did not. All we need is reasonable doubt and you cannot walk away as the victor of this debate. I'm sorry, that's the way debate works.

As for my question, Paul, I think this issue of the death of Jesus is crucial in this debate. The issue of professional medical opinions has come up this evening. In your opening statement, you claimed that when a victim was crucified, the cause of death was usually asphyxiation. I think there may be a problem with that assessment. But before I mention it, would you describe for us how a person on a cross would have died of asphyxiation?

Paul: Imagine you have had a rather large spike nailed through your feet and one through each of your hands.

Moderator: Hold on a minute. Studies on cadavers have revealed that a person's hands cannot support the weight of a person. So if the nails had been inserted in the palms as you are suggesting, the weight of the body would not be supported by the hand, and the nail would tear through it. So how could a person have had his hands nailed?

Paul: You're correct. I should clarify that the Greek word for hand can mean anywhere on the arm.[3] Tap the underside of your wrist about where you are wearing your watch, and you'll notice a nerve tingle that feels a lot like hitting your funny bone. That is where most scholars believe a person was nailed.

Imagine you are nailed to a cross or a tree. Gravity naturally places the weight of your body on your feet, and this causes unimaginable pain. In order to take as much pressure as possible off of your feet, you slump in a downward position on the cross, allowing the nails in your hands or wrists to support the weight of your body. The problem is, when you are in this slumped position, you cannot breathe well. Over the years, hanging a person by their arms has been used as a means of torture for this very reason.[4] Breathing becomes shallow and difficult. Moreover, inhaling is easier than exhaling. So you have two major problems: it's hard to get enough air, and it's even more difficult to exhale. The result is that you're deprived of oxygen, and carbon dioxide builds up in your lungs. Too much and you die. Not enough oxygen and too much carbon dioxide—that is what you call asphyxiation.

In order to avoid asphyxiation on the cross, every few minutes you would have to push up on your pierced feet, exhale, and drop back down in order to take your weight off of your feet. After you were on the cross for a while, if the Romans wanted to expedite your death, they would break your legs so you could not push up any longer, and you would die of asphyxiation within a few minutes, no more than twelve.[5]

Moderator: Well, this is where my problem arises. You were there. You saw crucifixions, probably many of them. But from our position, we cannot be assured that either you or Muhammad is telling us all of the truth. That's why we need more evidence. A few physicians have shown that if a person's arms were straight out from their side at ninety degrees when crucified, asphyxiation would not be a threat. In fact, one physician named Fred Zugibe demonstrated that a person's arms could be a little higher, or at as much as sixty to seventy degrees, and asphyxiation still would not be a problem.[6]

Paul: Yes. But when you raise the arms a little higher, let's say to forty-five degrees or less, asphyxiation definitely becomes a problem. Breaking the legs of the victim in order to expedite death makes sense if asphyxiation was the usual cause of death. It does not make sense if asphyxiation is not a problem.[7]

Moderator: Muhammad, I'd like to ask you about the substitution theory of what happened to Jesus. A number of guesses have been made concerning *who* was actually substituted for Jesus. The *Gospel of Barnabas* reports that Judas was made to look like Jesus, whom he had just betrayed.[8] Others have said that it was Simon of Cyrene, who carried the cross of Jesus. What do you make of these?

Muhammad: The Qur'an does not specify who was substituted for Jesus, on whom be peace. So over the years people have made guesses. You should know too that not all Muslims hold that the *Gospel of Barnabas* is an authentic Gospel from Barnabas, one of Paul's traveling companions.

Paul: The *Gospel of Barnabas* has all kinds of problems that challenge its authenticity.[9]

Muhammad: Yes, but it does not matter, Paul. I did not use the *Gospel of Barnabas* in my argument against the resurrection of Jesus, peace be upon him. I think you've climbed up on a different hill!

[At this comment there is great laughter in the stadium.]

Moderator: Fair enough. But the substitution view seems unfalsifiable. No matter what evidence is against it, one could always attribute that evidence to Allah's effectiveness in making it appear that Jesus had been killed on the cross.

Muhammad: Yes. And this is a matter of faith in the glorious Qur'an. I have this faith because I know it is from Allah.

Furthermore, we must make historical considerations as well. If Paul can do this with the New Testament, I can do it with the Qur'an. Islam has no problem with a prophet being killed. Islam has no problem with God raising a prophet from the dead. Thus the Qur'an would have no reason to say otherwise regarding these matters. That the Qur'an reports that Jesus was not killed on a cross would seem to be evidence for its truth. Besides, it does not matter for this debate, since in reality I do not have to defend any Muslim position. For me to win, I need only to show that the resurrection of Jesus, on whom be peace, does not look likely. Paul is the one who has the burden to show that Jesus rose from the dead. If he fails at doing this, he loses.

Paul: I would like to make a comment related to substitution theories. These did not originate with Islam. The Gnostics started positing these as early as the first part of the second century, or within one hundred years of Jesus. They were the ones who first suggested that Simon of Cyrene was substituted.[10] From a non-supernatural point of view, Muhammad may have had contact with Arabian Christians out of Syria who embraced Gnostic substitution views.[11] In fact, this may have been the main form of Christianity familiar to Muhammad, although it was regarded as heretical by the majority of Christians.

So we should not embrace a view that the Qur'an had supernatural origins when a good natural theory is available to us. Besides, if Simon of Cyrene had been substituted, why don't we hear anything about what happened to him after he carried Jesus's cross? If he was made to look like Jesus, substituted, and killed, he'd no longer be around. Why doesn't anyone ask where he went? Why isn't there a story describing how God rewarded him? These are completely absent from the Gospels and early church traditions.

Moderator: But you don't know if Muhammad was familiar with a Gnostic form of Christianity.

Paul: I cannot be certain. But data exists that suggests that is the case. For example, read what the Qur'an says regarding Jesus's creation of live birds out of clay:

> And (appoint him) a messenger to the Children of Israel, (with this message): "I have come to you, with a Sign from your Lord, in that I make for you out of clay, the figure of a bird, and breathe into it, and it becomes a bird by Allah's leave."[12]

Elsewhere the Qur'an says:

> Then will Allah say: "O Jesus the son of Mary! Recount My favour to thee and to thy mother. Behold! I strengthened thee with the holy spirit, so that thou didst speak to the people in infancy and in maturity. Behold! I taught thee the Book and Wisdom, the Law and the Gospel. And behold! thou didst make out of clay, the figure of a bird, by My leave, and thou didst breathe into it, and it becometh a bird by My leave."[13]

Compare this to an apocryphal Gospel, a false Gospel written hundreds of years before the Qur'an:

> When this child Jesus was five years old, he was playing by the ford of a stream; and he gathered the flowing waters into pools and made them immediately pure. These things he ordered simply by speaking a word. He then made some soft mud and fashioned twelve sparrows from it. It was the Sabbath when he did this. A number of other children were also playing with him. But when a certain Jew saw what Jesus had done while playing on the Sabbath, he left right away and reported to his father, Joseph, "Look, your child at the stream has taken mud and formed twelve sparrows. He has profaned the Sabbath!" When Joseph came to the place and saw what had happened, he cried out to him, "Why are

you doing what is forbidden on the Sabbath?" But Jesus clapped his hands and cried to the sparrows, "Be gone!" And the sparrows took flight and went off, chirping. When the Jews saw this they were amazed; and they went away and reported to their leaders what they had seen Jesus do.[14]

Does this sound familiar? This is from the *Infancy Gospel of Thomas*, a book written in the middle of the second century or later. This story is not found in the earlier Gospels. But we find a variation of it in the Qur'an, five hundred years later.

Muhammad: I'm glad you read both the passages from the Qur'an and from the *Infancy Gospel of Thomas*. Notice that there are more differences than similarities! In the Qur'an, Jesus forms a bird out of clay, breathes on it, and it becomes alive. In the *Infancy Gospel of Thomas*, he forms not one but twelve sparrows out of clay, does this on the Sabbath, breaking the Law, and claps his hands instead of breathing on it, and the sparrows fly off making noise.

Paul: The story is close enough, however, that a common source is likely.

Muhammad: And which is closer to that common source? All of the extra detail appears in the *Infancy Gospel of Thomas*, not the Qur'an. Therefore, I think this is good evidence that the story came from Allah as it actually occurred.

Paul: Not at all. The account of Jesus turning clay to living birds does not appear in any early accounts, which hurts the credibility of both the *Infancy Gospel of Thomas* and the Qur'an. Moreover, this story of the clay bird is not alone in the Qur'an as this type of story. Sura 5:110, which I already quoted, says that while a babe in the cradle Jesus spoke as articulately as an adult.[15] Again, the earliest sources contain no reports of this. If this had truly occurred, why didn't Matthew and Luke report it in their extensive narratives of Jesus's birth? They would have no reason to omit it. These accounts of the infant Jesus talking as an adult and the young boy Jesus making clay birds come to life is the kind of fiction we find in *The Last Temptation of Christ* and *The Da Vinci Code*. It does not bear any resemblance to the real Jesus.

Muhammad: If Jesus performed miracles as an adult, why not as a child? If he could be born of a virgin, then why not talk as an infant? If you believe one, why not the other? You are inconsistent, Paul!

Paul: The problem with these accounts is not that they could not occur. The problem is that there is no evidence that they did. Merely citing two sources, one that was written more than one hundred years after Jesus and the other that was written about six hundred years after Jesus and is fifth-hand testimony at best, does not provide anything that would impress a historian.

Muhammad: I am not here to impress a historian, Paul. I am only interested in serving Allah. If Allah says something in the Qur'an, I believe it, even if every historian says "no." But I have no idea where you are getting this idea that the Qur'an is fifth-hand testimony. It is firsthand. I heard it directly from angel Gabriel.

Paul: Even if I were to believe that it was Gabriel who revealed the Qur'an to you, that is secondhand testimony for you only. For those in the twenty-first century it is fifth-hand testimony.

Muhammad: How do you arrive at the conclusion that it is secondhand? I am an eyewitness to the revelation passed on to me by Gabriel.

Paul: Yes. It was passed on to you. The actual Qur'an is supposed to be in heaven. Correct?

Muhammad: Yes. That is correct.

Paul: Today, if we could read the Qur'an in heaven, then we would have firsthand testimony. We can't. Instead, you say it was communicated by Gabriel. If we could hear it directly from Gabriel as you did, that would be secondhand testimony. We can't. Then you passed it on to others. If we could have heard it directly from you, that would be third-hand testimony. People in the twenty-first century can't. Since you were illiterate, you passed it along to others who committed it to memory or wrote it down. If we could hear directly from them or read what they wrote, that would be fourth-hand testimony. We can't. Islamic tradition says that not until fourteen to twenty years after your death were the Qur'anic revelations collected into a single volume that is the standard volume we have today. If we can read that volume, and perhaps we can if the questionable Islamic tradition is true, that is fifth-hand testimony.

Muhammad: Even if you are correct, Paul, Allah can certainly preserve his word, even in fifth-hand testimony.

Paul: I could not agree more. Whether he has is another question. But you must note that the Qur'an as it is read in the twenty-first century, even in Arabic, is at best fifth-hand testimony.

Moderator: Then, Paul, neither do you have firsthand testimony when it comes to the New Testament.

Paul: In many cases we do. For example, there are my writings.

Moderator: Yes. But when we are discussing the appearances of Jesus after his death, you were an eyewitness. When we read your writings regarding the appearance of Jesus to you, that's secondhand testimony for us.

Paul: Yes. I agree.

Moderator: And let's say the creed in 1 Corinthians 15 is from the original disciples. That's thirdhand testimony because we did not see Jesus's appearance to them. Their testimony is secondhand. Your record of the creed is third-hand to us. And if the creed is a result of someone formalizing the testimony of the original disciples, we have fourth-hand testimony. So we have the appearances, the disciples, the creed, and then you telling us. That's fourth-hand testimony and almost the same as what you're saying about the Qur'an.

Paul: Yes and no. Remember that you heard it from my writings. So that's secondhand, not fourth. Regarding the creed being as much as fourth-hand: yes. However, there is a huge difference. The message contained in the creed in 1 Corinthians 15 which you allude to can be corroborated by other data that is relatively early, whereas the reports in the Qur'an cannot. For example, the creed reports the resurrection appearances of Jesus to others. This is corroborated in my writings, for example, when I say that the disciples and I were proclaiming the same thing concerning the resurrection of Jesus.[16] Elsewhere I reported how I set the message I was proclaiming before the leading apostles in Jerusalem: Peter, James, and John. This message included Jesus's resurrection, and they approved it.[17] The book of Acts likewise reports how the other apostles were proclaiming Jesus's resurrection and appearances.[18]

Now when we come to the Qur'an, we have no such corroboration. It is a single book. If you want to claim that the *hadith* confirms the process by which the Qur'anic revelations were collected into a single volume that is pure, you must keep in mind that the earliest *hadith* appears more than two hundred years after Muhammad. Thus, here's a simple comparison: the New Testament material on Jesus's resurrection is fourth-hand testimony at worst, although some of its writers gave firsthand testimony. It was written between two and seventy years after the event and corroborated between twenty-seven and seventy years later. The Qur'an is fifth-hand testimony. It was written fourteen to twenty years after the revelation to Muhammad and corroborated at least two hundred years later.

So historically speaking, the New Testament accounts of Jesus have a much higher quality to them than the Qur'an has concerning the message it provides.

Moderator: And we are going to end this part of our discussion on the death of Jesus at this time. You have heard the arguments and replies. Paul has said there is good historical evidence for Jesus's death by crucifixion, that all of Muhammad's objections fail, and that his evidence for the Qur'an's being from God is not good. Muhammad has argued that there are reasons for doubting Jesus's death and that the Qur'an is from Allah and is trustworthy on the matter when it says that Jesus did not die on the cross.

Let's move on to a new topic: the empty tomb.

10

Discussion Period: Part Five

Moderator: Muhammad, this question is for you. One of Paul's reasons for believing that Jesus's tomb was empty is that the Roman and Jewish authorities would only have had to exhume the body and parade it through the streets of Jerusalem for all to see and the scandal would have been exposed. But apparently they were unable to do this. What do you do with that?

Muhammad: Yes. I think this is a horrible reason for believing in the empty tomb. According to the New Testament, when was the first time Jesus's disciples proclaimed the resurrection of Jesus?

Moderator: About fifty days after his crucifixion.

Muhammad: Yes. Fifty days. Think of what a corpse looks like after fifty days. It has decomposed severely. And what Jew would want to touch it and become ritually impure? So no Jew would touch it in order to exhume it, and even if they did, it would have already decomposed beyond recognition. Therefore, this is not at all a good reason for believing the tomb was empty.

Paul: If the Jews could get the Romans to kill someone for them, why not get them to exhume a harmless corpse for them too?

Muhammad: Paul, you earlier noted how Josephus reported that Jews in Jerusalem removed the bodies of the crucified from their crosses by sunset and buried them. If they did this for religious reasons, do you think they would really exhume that body and display it publicly?

Paul: If the Jews wouldn't, why not the Romans?

Muhammad: The Romans allowed the Jews in Jerusalem to remove corpses from crosses for religious purposes. So they were flexible to accommodate their religious practices. They were not going to do something as provocative as parading a corpse through the streets of Jerusalem. Not only would the Jews have rioted over such an atrocity but Jesus, upon whom be peace, had a lot of followers in Jerusalem. The situation would have been too volatile to do such a thing.

Paul: Perhaps they would not have dragged the body through the streets of Jerusalem. However, all that the Jewish or Roman authorities would have had to do was go to the tomb, open it, see Jesus's body, and tell others it was still there. But not a single account exists where it was claimed that his corpse was still in the tomb. Instead, the opposition attempted to account for why the tomb was empty—they said his disciples had stolen the body.

Moderator: And what about the fact that Jesus's corpse would not have been recognizable by the time word was spreading that his tomb was empty?

Paul: That's not true. One of your scholars questioned a medical examiner about this in the United States.[1] At the time, he lived in Virginia, where the climate is quite humid. The medical examiner noted that in humid climates, bodies will tend to decompose much more quickly than in arid ones like Jerusalem. Yet even in Virginia, after fifty days of decomposition, a person's stature, hair, and profound wounds such as one would receive from crucifixion would certainly be noticeable. Had Jesus's corpse been exhumed, this would have been enough to cause great doubt among Christians, and a great exodus from the Christian faith would have occurred. This exodus would have to be explained by Christian apologists of the second and third centuries. But there is no hint that any such exodus occurred.

Moderator: Paul, let's say that the body was removed from the cross and buried by sunset as Josephus reported was the custom in Jerusalem. How can we be certain that the location of the tomb used by Joseph was known by the early Christians? You see, if it wasn't, then I think a possibility exists that the early Christians visited the wrong tomb, discovered it empty, and concluded Jesus had been raised.

Paul: Well, it's important to remember that, as I shared in my rebuttal, an empty tomb would not have convinced skeptics that Jesus had been resurrected. People like James and me would have been the first to suspect that the body had been stolen or that the wrong tomb had been visited. Second, even if the earliest Christians had gone to the wrong tomb, we would have expected the authorities to check the correct tomb. And if the corpse was still there, news of this would have been spread. Instead, the report that went out was that Jesus's disciples had stolen his body, which seems to have been an attempt to account for a missing corpse.

Moderator: And how do we know that the body wasn't stolen? How do we know that the Jewish leaders were not in fact telling the truth when they said that Jesus's disciples had stolen his body?

Paul: There are several reasons to reject that theory. For one, my colleagues, who were the disciples, were all willing to suffer continuously and even die for their beliefs that Jesus had been raised. How do we explain this if they had stolen the body? People are often willing to suffer and die for what they believe is true. But I think it is really straining it to say that all of them were willing to suffer and die for what they knew was a false report. Liars make poor martyrs.

Second, I would not have been convinced by an empty tomb. I would have been the first to suspect theft on their part. But I became a Christian because I saw the risen Jesus with my own eyes. Neither would the skeptic James have converted merely because of an empty tomb. My point is, the theory that Jesus's disciples stole his body can only account for the empty tomb. It cannot account for the other known facts, and therefore, it is not a good theory.

Muhammad: The Qur'an also accounts for all of the facts you've asserted except the death of Jesus, on whom be peace, which as we have seen is no fact at all.

Paul: The Qur'an does not account for the facts nearly as well as the theory that Jesus rose from the dead. If someone was substituted for Jesus, was crucified in his place and buried, there is no reason to believe his tomb would have turned up empty a few days later. Only if you hold that Allah allowed Jesus to be crucified and then made it appear that he had died, had him removed from his cross prematurely, buried him in a tomb, and then raised him can you hold the empty tomb. But that theory makes Jesus out to be a false prophet, since he predicted he would be killed. And there is no evidence for it anyway. It also does not account as well for the appearances, since the earliest proclamation is that Jesus was raised *from the dead*. Why say this if he didn't die?

Moderator: Well, they could have thought Jesus had died. If the Qur'an provides an accurate report of what happened and we hold the view that God allowed Jesus to look as though he were dead, that would have fooled his followers as well. So, naturally, when they saw him alive afterward, they thought he had been raised *from the dead*.

Paul: And Jesus never corrected them by setting them straight? Why not simply tell them God had rescued him and that he had never died? Why allow them to preach the resurrection of Jesus from the dead and wait six hundred years to set the record straight?

Muhammad: Your question assumes the appearance accounts are accurate, and I have shown that they are not.

Moderator: Let's come back to our discussion of the empty tomb. Then we'll return to the appearances in a few minutes. Paul, what do you do with the contradictions in the Gospel accounts of Jesus's resurrection? Matthew and Mark say there's one person at the tomb, whereas Luke and John claim there are two. Both can't be correct. Mark and Luke say the messenger was a man, whereas Matthew and John claim it was an angel.

Paul: You're on another hill again. You're talking about the Gospels, sources that are decades after the sources I appealed to. Remember, the *hadith* certainly contains some legends. Muslims acknowledge this, yet they don't use this to conclude that the Qur'an contains legend. Why not? Because the Qur'an predates the *hadith*, not the other way around. The Gospels do not predate the oral traditions or my writings. They were written afterward. So the point I've been trying to make this entire debate is this: even if everything Muhammad is saying about the Gospels is correct, it no more undermines the data I've provided for Jesus's resurrection than legend in the *hadith* calls into question the purity of the Qur'an.

Moderator: But without the Gospels, we don't know much about Jesus's resurrection, only that the early disciples were saying that he had risen from the dead.

Paul: We also know that they were willing to suffer continuously and die for those claims, which indicates that they truly believed what they were claiming. In addition, none of the three arguments I provided for the empty tomb rely on the Gospels. Plus, none of my arguments for Jesus's death rely on the Gospels.

Moderator: Well, let's take a moment and look at what you just said. Your first argument for the empty tomb was the Jerusalem factor, that Jesus's resurrection could not have been proclaimed in Jerusalem if the tomb had been occupied. But where do we hear that Jesus's resurrection was proclaimed in Jerusalem? The Gospels and Acts. You cannot get away from the Gospels, Paul, and that's why they are important in our discussion.

Paul: Tacitus is considered to be the greatest of Roman historians. Notice what he wrote:

> Christus, the founder of the name [Christian], had undergone the death penalty in the reign of Tiberius, by sentence of the procurator Pontius Pilatus, and the pernicious superstition was checked for a moment, only to break out once more, not merely in Judaea, the home of the disease, but in the capital [Rome] itself, where all things horrible or shameful in the world collect and find a vogue.[2]

Jerusalem is located in Judea. So Tacitus reports that when Jesus was crucified by Pilate, Christianity was stopped for a short period of time before it not only started up again where it had begun, in Judea, but also spread beyond the region. Isn't this precisely what the Gospels and Acts report? And here we have a non-Christian source testifying much the same thing. We cannot be certain that the "pernicious (or destructive) superstition" to which Tacitus refers is Jesus's resurrection. However, what can be said is that Tacitus's report is consistent with what the Gospels report.[3]

I also implied in my letters that the church was headquartered in Jerusalem.[4] Luke corroborated the same in Acts.[5] Thus, since Jesus's resurrection was the central teaching of the church, which had a strong presence in Jerusalem, then of course it was proclaimed there. The Gospels and Acts actually corroborate what I already implied earlier in my letters, and the report by Tacitus is consistent with further details concerning what the Gospels said occurred. This is strong support that Jesus's resurrection was proclaimed in Jerusalem. Accordingly, the logic behind the Jerusalem factor is valid.

Justin and Tertullian attest that the Jewish leadership was still claiming in their day that the disciples had stolen Jesus's body, and this was one hundred twenty to one hundred seventy years after Jesus's crucifixion. And it is well documented that *resurrection* involves the body that had died.[6] So, you see, all of my three facts can be established without even using the Gospels. Thus, attacking the Gospels does not undermine the data I provided.

Moderator: But it almost looks as if you're embarrassed by the Gospels and you're trying to avoid the issues.

Paul: Not at all! I'm only trying to keep our discussion focused on the issues relevant to our debate. Regarding the instances you cited, they aren't problems at all, even when we focus on the Gospels. For example, let's suppose that you're involved in a car accident and a friend is in the car with you. Two police officers show up a few minutes later. They approach you, and one begins asking some questions. When recalling the event later to some friends, you may tell them about the police officer who asked you questions, while the friend who was with you in the car at the time may note that there were two officers. There is no contradiction. One is simply providing more details than the other.

Regarding whether it was a man or an angel who appeared to the women, the man or men described by Mark and Luke are wearing white or shining clothes, which are often the marks of a heavenly visitation in the New Testament.[7] Moreover, angels are referred to as men and young men in ancient Jewish literature.[8] In fact, this takes place in Luke 24:4 where they are referred to as "men." Then just a few verses later in 24:23, they are referred to as "angels." These are not contradictions.

Muhammad: But Paul, you never answered my objection that some Christian scholars believe that the angels who appear in the empty tomb accounts in the Gospels are not real at all. Rather, angels were a common literary device in antiquity meant to say to the reader that God acted here in history. So we have to determine what is meant to be understood as history and what is meant to be understood as metaphor. This makes a huge difference.

For example, Paul, in four of your letters you refer to the church as the "body of Christ."[9] So when you speak of the resurrection of Jesus's body, this certainly can be understood as the church dying when Jesus died—even Tacitus confirms this as you pointed out earlier—and then the resurrection of Jesus, on whom be peace, could simply mean that he is not dead but alive here on earth because his teachings and power continue on in the church, his "body." For all we know, the appearances you mentioned could all be metaphors for the continuing power of Christ in their lives after he had been crucified. No literal appearance need be meant. So this accounts for both the empty tomb and the appearances. Since you cannot prove the death of Jesus, on whom be peace, you do not have anything in terms of evidence for his resurrection. Nothing!

Paul: When you assault the resurrection accounts in the Gospels, you are attacking one hill, Muhammad, while I'm on a different one. Nowhere did I appeal to the Gospels in my case for Jesus's resurrection, except on one occasion to describe James before he became a Christian. And I showed that the reports concerning this are historically reliable. So whether the angels were real is irrelevant.

However, I'm amazed that you would claim that angels were a common literary device in antiquity and not meant to be understood as real. Who did you claim delivered the Qur'anic revelations to you? An angel! Was this a common literary device too? In arguing in this manner against the Gospels, you have actually cast doubt on the Qur'an!

Muhammad: A thousand times no! You distort my words. I did not say that I thought of the angel in this manner. As you earlier noted, I first suspected that I was possessed by demons when I began receiving revelation. What I said, Paul, and you must listen more carefully, is that your own scholars suggest that this is the case with the Gospels.

Paul: I thought you didn't care what scholars think. Or is it that you only care when they're critical of my view? Some scholars may believe that the angels were literary devices. Certainly not all scholars hold this. We would have to look at their reasons for holding that and see if their position is more likely to be true than not. I am sorry if I took your statement out of context. I did not mean to. My point is this: even if the angels are apocalyptic literary devices inserted by the authors in order to alert the reader that God acted in the event described, that would only indicate that the authors were communicating that God was the cause of the empty tomb. It wouldn't follow that the tomb itself wasn't empty.

Muhammad: What about your references to the Christian church as the "body of Christ"? This is certainly a metaphor used in the New Testament. So why not in reference to the resurrection?

Paul: Such an explanation cannot account for all of the evidence for Jesus's resurrection. For example, let us suppose for a moment that you are correct. This would hurt my third argument for the empty tomb, that the concept of resurrection is something that occurs to the body. Why? Because if the metaphor of the "body of Christ" is used to refer to the continuing power and presence of Jesus in his church, it need not refer to a literal event that occurred to Jesus's body. But this metaphor theory cannot explain why the authorities simply did not expose the actual body of Jesus, or why members of the Jewish leadership were claiming that the disciples of Jesus had stolen his body, or why Celsus in the second century attempted to explain away the empty tomb by saying Jesus and his followers were involved in "a conspiracy."[10] Furthermore, if this was a common literary device as you suggest, why do skeptics of that day respond to the claims concerning Jesus's resurrection as though they were intended to be understood as historical rather than metaphorical? Since I used the metaphor of the "body of Christ," I certainly was familiar with this literary device. Would I have given up my Jewish beliefs and converted to the faith I had sought to destroy merely because I liked a certain metaphor? Do you think the skeptic James, who was a pious Jew, would do this too? It just becomes far too much of a strain to hold such a view.

Muhammad: The problem I have with what you just said is that you are picking and choosing what fits your view while neglecting to mention what you wrote elsewhere that supports the metaphorical view. I want you to observe what you wrote in your first letter to the Corinthian church in your famous resurrection chapter. Let me read chapter 15, verses 42 through 47:

> So also is the resurrection of the dead. It is sown in a corruptible state, it is raised in incorruption; it is sown in dishonor, it is raised in glory; it is sown in weakness, it is raised in power; it is sown a natural body, it is raised a spiritual body. If there is a natural body, there is also a spiritual body. So also it is written, "The first man, Adam, became a living soul." The last Adam became a life-giving

spirit. But, the spiritual is not first, but the natural; then the spiritual. The first man is from the earth; the second man is from heaven.

I find two of your statements to be of special interest. When contrasting our present state of existence with how it will be, you say we are buried in the ground as *natural* beings and we will be raised as *spiritual* beings. The New Revised Standard Version renders verse 44: "It is sown a physical body, it is raised a spiritual body. If there is a physical body, there is also a spiritual body." In other words, what we now have is a physical body, and what we will have is a spiritual body.

This fits very nicely with the metaphorical view, since you are clear in your own words that you do not believe in a physical resurrection body. The resurrection body will be a spiritual one. And since you believed this about the resurrection bodies of Christians, you must have believed the same regarding the body of Jesus, on whom be peace, since just a few verses earlier you wrote, "But now Christ has been raised from the dead, the first fruit of those who are sleeping [or who have died]."[11]

Paul: You misunderstand what I meant by the term *natural*. The New Revised Standard Version and its predecessor the Revised Standard Version are the only translations to use the word *physical*. Virtually every other translation renders the word *natural*.[12] Those who translate the word as *physical* are mistaken, and it is easy to demonstrate this.

The Greek word we are talking about is *psychikos*.[13] Would you like to know how many times in the Bible, including the intertestamental writings, this word means *physical* or *material*, as the New Revised Standard Version suggests? Zero! It is never used that way.[14] The Greek word we are talking about for *spiritual* is *pneumatikos*.[15] Would you like to know how many times this word means *im-*

(127)

material as the New Revised Standard Version suggests? Zero![16]

To see what I meant by these words, you only need to look a few chapters earlier in my same first letter to the Corinthian church. In chapter 2, verses 14 and 15, I wrote:

> But a *natural* man does not accept the things of God's Spirit, for they are foolishness to him; and he is not able to understand them, for they are *spiritually* discerned. But the *spiritual* one discerns all things.

I'm saying here that the natural man who is controlled by his fleshly and sinful desires does not accept the truths of God because they can only be understood by those who are controlled by desires that are centered on the true God—in other words, spiritual people. Thus, in chapter 15, verse 44, I'm saying that our bodies are buried with all of their fleshly and sinful appetites. But they are raised with only holy appetites that are focused on God. There is no reason whatsoever for translating what I wrote to mean that we are buried with physical bodies but will be raised with immaterial ones, leaving the old body in the ground.

Moderator: Then what did you mean when you said in the next verse that Jesus is a "life-giving spirit"?

Paul: Notice what I wrote and the words that I used:

> So also it is written, "The first man, Adam, became a living soul."[17] The last Adam became a life-giving spirit.

The Greek words I use for *soul* and *spirit* in this verse are root words for the words *natural* and *spiritual* that we just discussed. So this pretty much rules out that I am here using *spirit* in the sense of something that is immaterial. But notice one other thing. In a letter to the church in Rome that I wrote about two years later, I said:

> But if the Spirit of the one who raised Jesus from the dead dwells in you, the one who raised Christ from the dead shall give life also to your mortal bodies through his Spirit who dwells in you.[18]

In this verse I say that the one who raised Jesus from the dead will also *give life* to the mortal bodies of Christians on the final day. So God's Spirit will give life to the Christian's mortal body. When we look back at 1 Corinthians 15:45, I refer to Jesus as a "life-giving spirit." I use the same Greek word for "life-giving" in 1 Corinthians 15:45 that I do for "give life" in Romans 8:11.[19] Not only is Jesus a spirit in the sense that everything about him is controlled by God, he is "life-giving" in the sense that as God gave life to Jesus's mortal body, God will give life to the mortal bodies of Christians.

Muhammad: No. You are wrong, Paul. In Romans 8:11 you said that *God's Spirit* will raise the mortal bodies of Christians from the dead even as he did the mortal body of Jesus. If in 1 Corinthians 15:45 you are saying that *Jesus* will give life to the mortal bodies of Christians when he raises them from the dead, you are contradicting yourself.

Paul: No, I'm not. You should understand that the earliest Christians recognized that the Father, Son, and Holy Spirit were three distinct persons who were all one God, not three. A number of times the Bible says in one passage that God will do something and in another that Jesus is the one who will do it or who did it. God and Jesus and the Holy Spirit seem to be used interchangeably at times.[20]

Muhammad: That is shirk[21] or blasphemy! The Qur'an is clear on this matter as I earlier stated:

O People of the Book! Commit no excesses in your religion: nor say of Allah aught but the truth. Christ Jesus the son of Mary was (no more than) a Messenger of Allah, and His Word, which He bestowed on Mary, and a Spirit proceeding from Him: so believe in Allah and His Messengers. Say not "Trinity": desist: It will be better for you: for Allah is One God: Glory be to Him: (Far Exalted is He) above having a son. To Him belong all things in the heavens and on earth. And enough is Allah as a Disposer of affairs.[22]

Elsewhere, Allah could not be clearer on this matter:

And behold! Allah will say: "O Jesus the son of Mary! Didst thou say unto men, 'Worship me and my mother as gods in derogation of Allah'?" He will say: "Glory to Thee! Never could I say what I had no right (to say). Had I said such a thing, Thou wouldst indeed have known it. Thou knowest what is in my heart, though I know not what is in Thine. For Thou knowest in full all that is hidden."[23]

Paul: It is blasphemy or shirk to refer to Jesus as God only if it's not true. If it's true, you and all Muslims are guilty of an equal sin, because you refuse to worship the true God as he is: one God in three persons. On this, I do not care what the Qur'an says. Let God be true and every man and false Scripture a liar![24]

A loud gasp of outrage is heard throughout the stadium as many Muslims are stunned and appalled to hear these words. Bowers recognizes that the situation could become volatile.

11

Discussion Period: Part Six

Moderator: We're getting way off track. Let's stay on topic, gentlemen. We have shifted our discussion onto the appearances. I would like to raise a few more questions on this topic. The Gospel of Matthew reports that after Jesus's resurrection, when he appeared to his disciples in Galilee, some worshiped him, while others doubted.[1] If Jesus had appeared in a physical, material body, Paul, why would any of his disciples doubt what they were seeing? This passage seems to describe the appearance more as a vision than as a bodily resurrection.

Paul: It doesn't at all suggest a vision. Remember that just a few verses earlier Matthew reported that the tomb was empty. An empty tomb suggests a bodily resurrection in the clearest of terms. He also says that when the women saw Jesus, they took hold of his feet.[2] That's physical.

A number of explanations for this verse do not at all strain the text and do not suggest a vision. For one, the others who doubted may have been not the disciples of Jesus but other Galileans who knew of Jesus. These may not have doubted that they were seeing a physical appearance of Jesus but rather that he had died. Consider that Galilee is a three-day journey from Jerusalem. Perhaps the scenario looked like this: Jesus has appeared in front of a great number of people in Galilee, and one Galilean says to another, "What's the big deal? He's been here before." The other says, "It's big because he was crucified in Jerusalem last Friday and, behold, he rose from the dead!" The first replies, "Yeah, right. You expect me to believe that? They probably killed someone who looked like him." Such a person would have doubted Jesus's resurrection because, like Muhammad, he would have doubted his death. This makes perfect sense of the passage. Other possible interpretations also exist.[3]

Moderator: So you're suggesting that Jesus's appearance in Galilee may have been to his disciples as well as to others. That is not what your colleague Peter said. In Acts 10:39–41 Peter is talking and says:

> We ourselves are witnesses of all the things he did in the land of the Jews and in Jerusalem. They killed him, hanging him on a tree. God raised him on the third day and granted that he become visible, not to all the people, but to witnesses who were chosen beforehand by God; those of us who ate and drank with him after his resurrection from the dead.

Peter said that he did not appear to everyone but only to those who were his disciples after his resurrection. That's very convenient, Paul. He only appeared to his disciples. Why not appear to many others if he wanted the entire world to believe, as it claims in the New Testament?[4]

Paul: Peter is not excluding others. Those "who ate and drank with him after his resurrection from the dead" may have included new converts. Peter is making a general observation that Jesus did not go around showing himself to everyone. The same author who reports Peter's words in Acts 10 likewise reports that after Jesus's resurrection and ascension into heaven, the disciples returned to Jerusalem and joined others in frequent prayer. These "others" included Jesus's women followers, his mother, and his brothers, the very brothers who were unbelievers during Jesus's ministry.[5] What do you think is the best explanation for their conversion? The same Luke also reports an appearance of Jesus to me three times in the same book.[6] I was anything but a follower of Jesus at the time. Why didn't he appear to thousands? I don't know. I do know this: he was quite effective in his method in getting the word out to others! Within three hundred years, the mighty Roman empire would be transformed by Christianity, and two thousand years later, nearly one-third of the world's people refer to themselves as Christian.

Muhammad: Let us consider the appearance on the Emmaus road. His own disciples did not recognize him. Why is it that if the body of Jesus, on whom be peace, that was buried is the same body that was resurrected, as you say, those who knew him didn't recognize him?

Paul: The report of Jesus's appearing on the Emmaus road says that they failed to recognize Jesus because "their eyes were kept from recognizing him"[7] and that they later recognized him when "their eyes were opened."[8] This sounds like they would have recognized him if their eyes had not been kept from doing just that.[9] The text also says the tomb was empty and that a physical and bodily Jesus walked and conversed with two of his followers.

Moderator: Paul, why aren't there any appearances reported by Mark's Gospel? Most scholars believe that Mark is the earliest Gospel. That Gospel ends with the empty tomb, an angel telling the women Jesus was raised, and the women running off fearful and telling no one. Then in Matthew, whose Gospel probably comes next, Jesus appears to the women, who go back and tell the disciples. Why is Mark's account so different? Almost all scholars agree that verses 9 through 20 of chapter 16 in Mark's Gospel were later added, since they are absent from the best manuscripts. So what happened to the ending, Paul? Was it cut out because Christians did not like what it said?

Paul: Scholars are quite uncertain regarding the ending of Mark's Gospel. Many believe that the original ending was lost for some unknown reason. The majority currently hold that Mark intended to end his Gospel abruptly at verse 8 with the women running off and telling no one.[10] Perhaps his readers who knew the entire story of Jesus's resurrection would have replied, "Ah! Yes! People need to tell of Jesus's resurrection, and *we* are those people!"[11]

Muhammad: Paul, you appeal to Clement of Rome. But I said his report is far too late. It is after Matthew, Mark, and Luke, about sixty-five years after the crucifixion. You said that since he knew the disciples, it does not matter how late he wrote. But you are wrong, Paul. Memories get corrupted over time, and we can expect that Clement's recollection of what he was told by the disciples wouldn't be perfect many years later.

Paul: Perhaps some details may be forgotten or remembered inaccurately. But he certainly would have remembered whether Peter and the other disciples had taught that Jesus had been resurrected from the dead. Now, if you are going to call Clement into question because he is writing sixty-five years after the event and thirty to thirty-five years after he heard the disciples teach these things, what do you do with the *hadith*? Bukhari didn't write until more than two hundred years after your death, Muhammad. So if you think thirty-five to sixty-five years is too late, you should not at all be satisfied with over two hundred years, and present-day Muslims will be forced to disregard all of the *hadith*.

Muhammad: The difference is that Bukhari thoroughly investigated the stories he reported. He was aware of the line of transmission back to the eyewitnesses of my life.

Paul: Clement and I both knew the original disciples of Jesus. We were their colleagues. We didn't need a line of transmission. In fact, since the original disciples were still alive, no line had been established. However, even about one hundred seventy years later, Tertullian reported that a register was kept in his day showing the line of transmission of the apostolic tradition.[12] In other words, a clear lineage back to the original apostles was available and it is far closer to the eyewitnesses than the *hadith*. So my point stands.

Muhammad: I know you wish to focus only on the earlier evidence like the *kerygma*, not the Gospels. So I'll do just that. You said the creed in 1 Corinthians 15:3–7 is one of the very earliest traditions. Correct?

Paul: Yes.

Muhammad: In that creed you provide a list of appearances: to Peter, to the Twelve, to over five hundred followers of Jesus at one time, to James, and to all of the apostles. Then, Paul, you add your own name to the list. In doing this you seem to equate your experience with the others'. So it is interesting to read about your experience in Acts.[13] There's a bright light in the sky, and a voice out of heaven speaks to you. If this is also what the others saw, it sounds much more like a vision than a bodily resurrection.

Paul: Jesus appeared to me after his ascension to heaven, whereas he appeared to the others *before* his ascension. So you can understand why the nature of his appearance to me was different. When I added my name to the list, I was not trying to equate the nature of my appearance to what the other apostles had experienced. I was saying that the risen Jesus had appeared to me too.[14]

(135)

I'm clear concerning the bodily appearances of Jesus elsewhere in Acts where Luke reports other things that I said. For example, in chapter 13 I contrast the risen Jesus with David, saying, "For David, on the one hand, served the purpose of God in his own generation, died, was laid with his ancestors, and he decayed. On the other hand, he whom God raised did not decay."[15]

I do not think I could have been any clearer that I was saying Jesus rose bodily from the dead. So you should take Luke's report of my conversion experience in light of other statements he reports me saying. Otherwise, you're involved in cafeteria criticism, where you walk through a buffet line and choose only what sounds good for your case when taken alone and ignore the other entrees that would upset your theory. This is especially damaging when I'm fairly clear in my own writings that Jesus rose bodily.[16]

Moderator: Acts 13:36–37 is an interesting passage, Paul, because in the verse that immediately precedes that passage, you quote Psalm 16:10 where the psalmist writes, "You will not allow your holy one to see decay."

Paul: Yes. We understood the resurrection of Jesus as a fulfillment of prophecy.

Muhammad: Or perhaps the early Christians strained passages in the Old Testament in order to make their false teachings more palatable to Jews of the day.

Paul: Some of the passages in the Old Testament that we cited are certainly clearer than others. For example, Psalm 22 and Isaiah 53 can be seen to refer to the crucified Jesus quite clearly and without strain. It could very well be that the psalmist was not intentionally predicting the resurrection of Jesus in Psalm 16:10. But that does not discount the possibility that God had it in mind. However you may look at it, you are still left with either a prediction of the resurrection or an event for which the earliest followers of Jesus were trying to find understanding from the Old Testament: his bodily resurrection.

Muhammad: I would like to look at some of the other early oral traditions for a moment. In Philippians 2:8–11, you wrote the following:

> And being found in appearance as a man, he humbled himself, becoming obedient to death, even death on a cross. Wherefore also, God exalted him, and gave him the name which is above every name, in order that at the name of Jesus every knee bows in heaven, and on earth, and under the earth, and every tongue confesses that Jesus Christ is Lord, to the glory of God the Father.

This hymn is among the very earliest Christian traditions. It mentions the death of Jesus but makes no mention of his resurrection. Perhaps some of Jesus's disciples believed he died and then appeared. They were not aware that God had healed him completely and then allowed him to appear. This fits in with a rescue theory better than a resurrection from the dead. And since you included it in your letter, of necessity it came before your letter. Thus we have early tradition that predates even you, Paul—a tradition that does not include the resurrection of Jesus.

Paul: Resurrection is not excluded in the hymn. It is Jesus's end state that is being emphasized—his glorification.

Muhammad: It does not say that. It says that he died and that God exalted him and gave him a name above all names. Resurrection is not even in the picture.

Paul: Resurrection does not have to be mentioned every time. It says God gave him not *"a* name" but *"the* name" that is above all names. It was already in existence. And what is the name God gave him? "Lord." Every tongue will confess "Jesus is Lord."

Moderator: What does that mean, "Lord"?

Paul: Look at my letter to the Romans, which I wrote just prior to my letter to the Philippians. In chapter 10, verse 9, I write, "If you confess with your mouth 'Jesus is Lord' and believe in your heart that God raised him from the dead, you will be saved."

This is also *kerygma*, and it uses the same grammatical structure, literally, "The Lord is Jesus." Skip down four verses to chapter 10, verse 13. There I cite Joel 2:32 which says: "Everyone who calls on the name of the Lord will be saved."

Joel was certainly referring to God when he wrote that. So when I quote it in relation to Jesus, calling "on the name of the Lord" and confessing "the Lord is Jesus," who do you think we early Christians thought Jesus was? God!

[Throughout the large stadium many Muslims begin yelling at Paul for this remark. After about ten seconds of much noise, Muhammad lifts his hand, motioning for silence, and a hush falls on everyone.]

Muhammad: Paul, what this shows is that you regarded Jesus as God. But it in no way shows this is what most of the early Christians believed.

Paul: You are the one who said that this hymn predates my letter to the Philippian church, that it is among the earliest Christian traditions, and that it didn't come from me because its author wasn't aware of Jesus's resurrection. Now you want to say it only shows what I believe. What is this double-talk?

Moderator: Again, I think we are getting way off the subject of Jesus's resurrection, so I'm going to pull us back on topic. Paul, I want to emphasize that I don't mean to appear to be picking on you. But you are the one making the positive assertion that Jesus rose from the dead, and so Muhammad is correct that the major burden of proof is on you. So you are going to get the majority of the questions. I want to ask you a question regarding the oral traditions, the *kerygma* that keeps coming up. How much of it mentions Jesus's death?

Paul: In the New Testament, there are thirty-four passages, all very early, dated between one to thirty-four years after Jesus's crucifixion, some of which are traceable to the earliest Christians—thirty-four passages which say that Jesus died or was resurrected.[17] Contrast this with a few passages which claim that Jesus did not die. The earliest of these comes from the Gnostics, about a century after the crucifixion of Jesus.[18] Historians would think it foolish to suggest accepting the later Gnostic accounts while rejecting the earlier and more numerous examples in the New Testament.

Discussion Period: Part Seven

Moderator: I have one last question for you, Paul, and it concerns your approach to arriving at historical conclusions. You say that the majority of scholars agree with your facts. That may be. But most don't believe that Jesus rose bodily from the dead. Why do you think that is, Paul?

Paul: That's a fair question. Reasons may vary from scholar to scholar. But in general I would say it is because they are hostile to the idea of the actual occurrence of a supernatural event. A debate on the subject of Jesus's resurrection was held in 1985 between Christian philosopher Gary Habermas and then atheist philosopher Antony Flew. Several scholars were asked to write a reply to be included in a book along with a transcript of the debate. One of the contributors was Charles Hartshorne whom the *Stanford Encyclopedia of Philosophy* describes as "one of the most important philosophers of religion and metaphysicians of the twentieth century."[1] Hartshorne wrote the following comment: "I can neither explain away the evidences to which Habermas appeals, nor can I simply agree with

Flew's or Hume's positions. . . . My metaphysical bias is against resurrections."[2]

Likewise, Sarah Coakley of Harvard admitted, "New Testament scholarship of this generation . . . is often . . . downright repressive—about supernatural events in general and bodily resurrection in particular."[3]

So I answer your question by saying I think the main reason scholars who grant the three facts I have presented feel comfortable in rejecting Jesus's bodily resurrection is not any lack of evidence. Rather, it is because they have a problem accepting the possibility of miracles. In other words, they have a philosophical objection, not a historical one.[4] But neither Muhammad nor I have any objection to the possibility of miracles.

Moderator: True, but make no mistake about it: you still have major philosophical differences. And your approaches to this topic of Jesus's resurrection from the dead differ significantly. Muhammad, I have a question for you that relates more to the death of Jesus than it does to his resurrection. According to Islam, many prophets have died. So why is there such a fuss over the possibility of Jesus's death on a cross?

Muhammad: Muslims have no problem with the death of prophets. If the Qur'an had stated that Jesus had died, Muslims would believe it. But in sura 4:157, the Qur'an clearly states that Jesus did not die on a cross. This is from Allah. Any fuss comes from Christians because they have the peculiar doctrine that Jesus died for the sins of mankind in order for redemption to occur. In fact, they argue that it had to occur this way. As a Muslim, I see no reason why things had to be this way. Nothing is impossible for Allah. So he can forgive sins without needing for someone to be brutally tortured and killed before he can do so. The thought that he would require a sinless, blameless person to suffer for someone else's sins is totally repugnant to Muslims. It does not make any sense to us.

Paul: That is because it is not within Islamic theology. However, this debate is not on how our theologies differ. It is on the facts, especially when it comes to Jesus's resurrection. If Jesus rose from the dead, Christianity is true and, accordingly, we have good reason for believing Christian theology over Islamic theology. So it is like I said in my opening remarks: if the evidence points to the historical event of Jesus's resurrection, it may be time to change your worldview and your theology if you are a Muslim.

Moderator: And whether Jesus rose from the dead is something that our viewers and readers will have to decide for themselves at this point. Thank you, gentlemen, for your participation in what has been a very invigorating and interesting debate that has challenged the rest of us greatly to think through what you both have said. I'm going to give each of you about five minutes to provide us with some final thoughts, and then I'll wrap things up with a few words of encouragement and admonition. Would the staff please bring up the podium once again?

Immediately the two men who removed the podium return it to its place. They then go over to the coffee table, pick it up, and take it offstage. Dr. Bahkr leans over toward Dr. Sweeney and says, "Bowers has been outstanding as a moderator. I don't think we could have chosen a better person for the job."

"I agree completely," Sweeney replies.

Bowers then turns to Muhammad and says, "Muhammad, you may go first."

13

Muhammad's Closing Statement

All praise goes to Allah, the most merciful and compassionate. I thank him for giving me the chance to speak once again on his behalf. I know that many of you are so very happy to see me. And I am very happy to see you too. Thank you for your very warm reception and for listening patiently to what I wanted to pass on to you. Although I am the last prophet of Allah, I am still a man. I brought you the truth once again today. After I am gone, you will still have the truth. It is the Qur'an. This book is the absolute revelation of Allah, praised be his name. I do not question the Qur'an, for I know it is from Allah, for he sent his angel Gabriel, who gave it to me.

We have heard a case for Jesus's resurrection from the dead this evening. Notice that Paul's case does not rely at all on what God said. Instead he relies on error-prone texts and what fallible and fickle scholars say. Many of them do not believe that God even exists, and if they do, they do not believe that he intervenes in our world. These are those whom Paul seems to respect this evening. Scholars change on their opinions. We can be certain that within one hundred years the consensus Paul refers to will no longer exist the same way. So his argument will not work at that time. On the other hand, the Qur'an never changes. You can rely on it today just as I relied on it in my day, fourteen hundred years ago.

Paul's case also relied on three facts: the death of Jesus by crucifixion, his empty tomb, and the beliefs of some friends and enemies that he had risen from the dead and appeared to them. But we saw very clearly that these are not facts at all. There are a number of reasons to doubt the reports—yes, even the early and eyewitness reports—that Jesus had been killed on the cross. First and primarily, we have the word of Allah himself in the Qur'an that says Jesus did not die on the cross. I explained how the Qur'an allows for two possibilities: someone was substituted for Jesus before he was crucified, or he was rescued by Allah during his crucifixion before he succumbed to death. Since Paul cannot show us conclusively that the Qur'an is unreliable on these matters, he cannot claim to have proven that Jesus died on the cross. And without certainty that Jesus died, we have far less certainty that he was resurrected, since the first requirement of a resurrection is that death occurred. So for all practical purposes, Paul lost tonight's debate. I could stop here. But I will go further just to make the matter clear to those who still doubt.

There is more—or really I should say there is less; that is, less certainty we can have regarding the death of Jesus. Paul gave us four reasons why we should believe Jesus died on the cross. But we saw that every one of those reasons is answered by Allah in his glorious Qur'an. First, he said that even a number of ancient non-Christian sources reported that Jesus died. I pointed out that if Allah made Jesus appear to be dead, of course they would have been fooled into believing he had died. Second, Paul argued that it was almost impossible for a person to survive crucifixion, and he is correct. But he believes God resurrected Jesus. Does he think resurrecting someone is less difficult than providing a substitution for or rescuing someone from the final consequences of crucifixion? Whether it is by a resurrection, rescue, or substitution, Allah overcomes any improbability. Nothing is too hard for Allah. Third, Paul argued that the opinion of most medical professionals is that Jesus died. But this is so easily explained that I should not have to. Just like Paul's second argument, if Allah wanted to keep Jesus from dying on the cross, he could have done it. Fourth and finally, Paul argued using Strauss's critique. However, I pointed out that if Allah provided a substitution for Jesus or rescued him, there would have been no need for the disciples to view him in a substantially wounded state. So the Qur'an has addressed every one of Paul's arguments, what he calls evidence. What I absolutely love about this is that one does not have to be a brilliant person to see the errors in Paul's arguments. One only has to believe the Qur'an. Allah provides all wisdom, and we praise him for doing that.

We also saw good reasons to doubt that Jesus's tomb was empty. Paul argued that if the body of Jesus still lay in the tomb, the enemies of Jesus would have exposed it to show he had not been raised. He further argued that the enemies of Jesus claimed that his tomb was empty. And finally he argued that since the definition of resurrection involves the bringing of the same body back to life, the New Testament writers must have meant that Jesus's body was raised when they referred to the event as his resurrection. Based on these three reasons, he concludes that the tomb must have been empty.

However, I pointed out that the empty tomb account is probably a legendary story that was invented years after Jesus's crucifixion, since the first time it is mentioned is in the Gospel of Mark, which was written around forty years after Jesus, a long enough time for stories to develop. Furthermore, Paul himself never specifically mentioned the empty tomb in his writings, not even in his famous chapter on resurrection, 1 Corinthians 15. Even if Jesus had been buried in a tomb, there is also the possibility that his followers went to the wrong tomb, saw that it was empty, and proclaimed that he had been resurrected. We should not believe the Gospels anyway. Their authors were biased and contradict one another, and we see an evolution of the resurrection story occurring before our very eyes when we read them. And some of what was reported concerning Jesus's resurrection was not intended to be understood literally. I also pointed out that an empty tomb is completely compatible with a rescue interpretation of the Qur'an in sura 4:157. Therefore, contrary to Paul's assertion, we can have no confidence, historically speaking, that Jesus's tomb was empty on the Sunday morning after his crucifixion.

We saw good reasons to doubt Paul's third fact: the appearances of the risen Jesus to others. The explanation in the Qur'an that Jesus was either rescued or someone was substituted for him easily accounts for any appearances that may have occurred. So there is no problem with their occurrence. Furthermore, Paul's evidence for the appearances is from him, and where it isn't, it is very late, even after the Gospels.

Remember that I could have stopped after I proved that we can have no confidence that Jesus died. But I went further to help those still doubting. And I did so using far fewer words than Paul throughout our debate. I could say much more, but I am almost out of time. As we have all seen, Paul's case is very weak, as it is very wrong. So the three facts that Paul's case rests upon are not facts at all. They do not hinder the Islamic viewpoint or its veracity.

I also provided a number of alternate explanations for Paul's three facts. If you think any one of them was an equally good if not better explanation, then Paul has failed to present a convincing case to you. I think that he has failed. Yes, he spoke with great eloquence and confidence. But that is how lies are normally packaged, are they not? Allah has given us the Qur'an in order to know the truth about him and what he wants. Following Allah is up to you. Allah will not force you. But if you refuse to obey the Qur'an, then I cannot be responsible for what happens to you in the end. Allah will be your enemy. He does not want that, because his nature is to be merciful and compassionate. However, if you reject him, he will not be humbled. It is you, his creation, who will be humbled.

I want to encourage my Muslim brothers and sisters to hold true to Allah. Islam is the true religion, and great reward awaits those who remain faithful to the end. You live in desperate times. But the Qur'an is correct when it says:

Do *men* think that they will be left alone on saying, "We believe", and that they will not be tested?

We did test those before them, and Allah will certainly know those who are true from those who are false.

Do those who practise evil think that they will get the better of Us? Evil is their judgement!

For those whose hopes are in the meeting with Allah (In the Hereafter, let them strive); For the Term (appointed) by Allah is surely coming: And He hears and knows (all things).[1]

Do not be deceived by Paul. He does not know Allah and does not speak on his behalf. He appeals to the seen

(149)

and to man's interpretation of it. The Qur'an has told us in advance that we will be tested. So even if a majority of scholars believe something that is contrary to what is written in the holy Qur'an, I am only impressed that the Qur'an is correct once again in predicting that very thing that questions it! These scholars do not know Allah. Even Paul himself wrote, "Though everyone else in the world is a liar, God is true. As the Scriptures say, 'He will be proved right in what he says, and he will win his case in court.'"[2] So let us side with Allah, and we will not be disappointed. Those who side with Paul will meet a humiliating end.

But I agree with Paul on one other thing: we must follow the truth. And since that truth is in the Qur'an, it is in everyone's best interests to be a Muslim.

Say: "There is no God but Allah. I will seek truth in Him, the Creator of all things."

For We created man and Jinn and We know what they proclaim.

Surely others deceive. But truth is found in Us. And We reveal it to whomever We will.

May the peace, mercy, and blessings of Allah be on all of his messengers and on those who follow him.

Muhammad smiles peacefully and begins to walk back to his seat. Twenty thousand Muslims applaud and yell praises to Allah at the top of their lungs while the Christians remain seated and watch silently. Dr. Bahkr stands and applauds but utters nothing. Dr. Sweeney smiles but remains seated. Bowers walks to the podium and says, "We will now hear closing comments from Paul."

14

Paul's Closing Statement

Again, I thank the Lord for allowing me to share the gospel with you today. How will each of you answer the question *Did Jesus rise from the dead?* Muhammad and I have proclaimed two different answers. Both of us claim to have had experiences with the divine. Muslims and Christians both claim that their Scriptures are inspired by God. And yet they cannot both be true since they disagree on the most major theological points. Did either Muhammad or I see a demon rather than a divine revelation? Did the New Testament or the Qur'an become corrupted along the way? How can you determine which is true and who is telling the truth? You have to look at the external evidence and ask which view, if any, fits the known facts. That's why I have been emphasizing the *historical* evidence during this debate and suggesting we must test our claims against the known facts. When you do this, the Qur'an fails to pass the test.

A prominent contemporary historian, N. T. Wright, comments: "What we are after is high probability; and this is to be attained by examining all the possibilities, all the suggestions, and asking how well they explain the phenomena."[1] In light of this, let us look now at our two theories this evening.

The Christian theory that Jesus was resurrected explains all of the evidence very well and without any strain. It easily explains Jesus's death by crucifixion. It easily explains the empty tomb. It easily explains the subsequent beliefs of many, friend and foe alike, that Jesus had been resurrected and had appeared to them. None of the data is strained in the least in order to arrive at the conclusion that Jesus rose from the dead. Moreover, all of the alternate explanations that have been proposed over the years, natural or even supernatural, have failed to explain all of the evidence. Muhammad thinks he succeeded in providing alternate explanations by citing the Qur'an. But citing what a single book says is not an adequate answer. Remember that it is a book that was written six hundred years after Jesus, and is fifth-hand at best, and shows signs of being influenced by Gnostic legend. It also seems to make claims that go against knowable historical facts. The Qur'an may have historical value insofar as it informs us of early Islamic beliefs. But when it comes to providing historical information on Jesus, it is unsalvageable. If Muhammad wants to believe it, he has the right to do so. It's his eternal soul that is on the line. For me, I'll go where the historical evidence points, and the resurrection of Jesus is the only plausible explanation for the known historical facts.

Now let us look at Muhammad's position: Jesus did not die on the cross, and without death there can be no resurrection. He offers two possibilities, rescue and substitution. But both of these theories have one major problem: there is no evidence for them. Let's look first at his rescue theory. It accounts for the empty tomb but has to strain to explain the evidence for the death of Jesus and his postresurrection appearances. In order to find support, the rescue theory has to strain to reinterpret the Gospel texts and accept texts that were written much later in history. It is based primarily on a single source that was written *six hundred years after Jesus*. I do not have to do this with Jesus's resurrection. I can look at all of the facts as they are. Muhammad is building castles in the air, so it should not be surprising when we do not feel obligated to rent a room.[2]

Not only does the rescue theory strain at and ignore the evidence; it is in fact contrary to all of the eyewitness testimonies to what happened to Jesus. The rescue theory likewise leads to the suggestion that the prophet Jesus was mistaken in his belief that he would soon die.[3] In doing so, this creates the possibility that Muhammad may have been mistaken concerning the source of the Qur'an. It actually opens the door to the Qur'an's origin being human or even demonic as Muhammad himself first suspected.

Thus, ironically, his attacks on Jesus's resurrection have served only to crack the foundations of his own belief system. It is as though he attacked a hill with a grenade, only to have it roll back down on him. In a similar vein, Solomon wrote, "If a man digs a pit, he will fall into it; if a man rolls a stone, it will roll back on him."[4]

What about his substitution theory, that Allah made someone to look like Jesus and the people who came to arrest him took that person instead? This theory suffers from even more problems because it accounts for even fewer of the known facts. In addition to being faced with virtually all of the same problems encountered by the rescue theory, substitution does not account for the empty tomb.

Muhammad challenged the reports of Jesus's resurrection. But his arguments are far too weak to support his conclusions. Given the strong evidence we have for the resurrection of Jesus, when we add that resurrection is the only plausible explanation that can account for the known historical facts regarding what happened to Jesus, we can have a high degree of confidence that this event occurred.

The conclusions I have presented this evening are based on strong historical evidence which even the majority of today's scholars grant. I never suggested we should accept the data simply because the majority of scholars do. Muhammad was correct when he stated earlier that many scholars do not believe Jesus rose from the dead. However, they do agree on the strength of the data on which my case is built. Scholars can be wrong, have been wrong in the past, and will be wrong many times to come. But that does not mean we should ignore them. Of course Muhammad wants to ignore them. I would too if I didn't have any evidence on my side. Remember, there are strong reasons for accepting the data I presented. These reasons are where I placed my focus. And I did not even mention that God's Holy Spirit provides assurance to the Christian that we believe the truth and belong to God: "The Spirit itself bears witness with our spirit that we are children of God."[5] I never brought this up as evidence because I can't prove it to someone who does not have that testimony from God. That would be like trying to convince a man who was born blind that grass is green.

Thus the major difference between the approach I took and the one Muhammad took is that I appealed to known historical evidence and showed how the Christian view fits perfectly, whereas Muhammad simply says that the Qur'an says it and that settles it for him. Well, that doesn't settle it for me or anyone who wants good evidence for the worldview on which they are basing their life and the eternal destiny of their soul.

The data points to the fact of Jesus's resurrection and away from the claims of Islam. Moreover, there are problems with our ability to know whether the Qur'an is true. Its own test is poor, and the historical evidence points to the death and resurrection of Jesus, indicating that the Qur'an is not the word of Allah and that Muhammad's first suspicions regarding its demonic origin may have been correct. The historical evidence further indicates that Jesus predicted his violent death. Thus if he did not die in that manner, he is a false prophet, contrary to the teachings of the Qur'an. But if he actually died a violent death as he predicted, the Qur'an is wrong for saying he did not. Either way, the Qur'an is wrong. So we should believe that Jesus rose from the dead unless there are compelling reasons to believe Islam. And we have not heard any this evening.

What we have heard very clearly is Muhammad's faith in the Qur'an. But that's not an argument that it is true. If Joseph Smith, the founder of Mormonism, were here before us, he would exhibit similar faith in the Book of Mormon. But such would hardly be a convincing argument. Granted, a few places in the Qur'an are intriguing in terms of statements carrying scientific implications. But the Bible contains these as well, and if we are honest, we must admit that for the most part these are not clear enough that we should base our worldview on them.

What we have heard from Muhammad is that we should believe that he heard from the angel Gabriel. But why should we when he himself was uncertain about it? Remember that for a while he thought he was being plagued by demons.

I will close with something I said in the first century:

> Therefore let it be known to you, brothers, that through this one [Jesus] the forgiveness of sins is proclaimed to you, and through this one [Jesus] everyone who believes is justified. . . . Beware, therefore, lest that which was spoken of in the prophets may not come upon you: "Look, you scoffers, and marvel, and be destroyed; for I myself am working a work in your days, a work which you will never believe, even if someone would describe it to you."[6]

All of us in this stadium, those watching this debate on television or computer, those listening by radio, and those reading a transcript—we all have been strongly influenced by what we have been taught since childhood. It is hard to break with the traditions of our parents who have loved us. I know what it is like. As one who commanded great respect among the Jewish leadership of my day, I lost everything when I became a Christian and became one whom they sought to kill. But I now regard everything I lost as waste, because what I gained in my relationship with the living God is so much greater![7] If those traditions we have been taught from our childhood conflict with God's truth, we must follow God rather than man. Jesus himself said:

> If you love your father or mother more than you love me, you are not worthy of being mine; or if you love your son or daughter more than me, you are not worthy of being mine. If you refuse to take up your cross and follow me, you are not worthy of being mine. If you cling to your life, you will lose it; but if you give it up for me, you will find it.[8]

We must ask God to show us the truth and ask him to give us the strength and the courage to step outside of our conditioning and seek the truth. I admonish you to give careful and serious thought to the issues involved. Do not simply reject the Christian position because it has large theological disagreements with Islam. Whichever religion is true, we should change our present theology in order to follow the truth.

We never need to fear the truth. We need to fear the possibility that we will not seek it thoroughly and honestly with an open mind and will then discover at our death that we have been committed to a false view. May God lead us all in our quest for the truth.

Paul returns to his seat as nearly twenty thousand Christians stand to their feet and let out the loudest applause of the evening. About ten Muslims seated in the upper deck stand up and begin to yell, "Away with the infidel!" Police officers move toward them quickly in order to remove them from the stadium should they begin to pose a threat. But the hecklers calm down and are seated. Dr. Sweeney and Dr. Bahkr turn back from looking at the section where the hecklers are seated and look at one another. They are speechless. Their eyes and open mouths communicate their thoughts: the program has been a success beyond all of their expectations. Bowers stands and walks to the podium. He looks around and begins to speak.

15

Moderator's Conclusion

I am pleased to be able to provide some closing comments. First I would like to summarize tonight's debate. Paul said that since there are two conflicting views on what happened to Jesus, each claiming to be the truth and to be reported in God-inspired Scriptures, one must consider the known historical facts in order to judge which view is correct. He then provided data for which he claims there is strong historical evidence: Jesus's death by crucifixion, his empty tomb, and the beliefs of a number of people that he had resurrected and had appeared to them. Paul's case for the resurrection of Jesus is that the theory that Jesus rose from the dead explains all of the evidence without any strain and that alternate theories, natural and supernatural alike, cannot do this. His conclusion is that Jesus's resurrection is the only plausible explanation for the known facts.

Muhammad's approach was completely different. He had absolute confidence that the Qur'an is the word of Allah. The Qur'an claims that Jesus did not die on the cross, and therefore, he could not have risen *from the dead*. Muhammad further argued that Paul's three knowable facts were refuted by the Qur'an and that as long as there is any reasonable doubt that Jesus died, there is reasonable doubt that he was resurrected. As long as reasonable doubt exists, one can say that Paul did not prove his case and therefore loses tonight's debate.

The question we all will have to answer as individuals is "Did Paul prove his case?" What did you think of his evidence? Did he present sound argumentation for the resurrection of Jesus? Did Muhammad's case based on the Qur'an really refute Paul's case? It may address Paul's arguments, but is there adequate strength behind Muhammad's assertion that the Qur'an is the word of Allah? Or is it merely an unsubstantiated claim? Do you employ historical facts to measure the accuracy of the Qur'an? Or do you use the Qur'an to measure the accuracy of what appear to be strongly evidenced historical facts? What did you think of Paul's criticisms of the Qur'an?

These are tough questions, and it is very easy for each of us to answer them according to our present religious persuasions without giving them serious thought. But this can be dangerous, at least for those on the wrong side. Many Muslims and Christians are very sincere about their faith. It is the most important thing in their lives. But they cannot both be correct. Therefore, at least one group is sincere and wrong.

Do not be confused by the rhetoric of Paul and Muhammad. They each have different styles that will appeal to different cultures. But rhetoric contributes nothing toward determining truth. You must look carefully at the arguments and the answers provided by each.

Lastly, although this debate is fictitious, the data presented in it is real and this calls for us to take it seriously.

Take an honest and thorough look at the facts.[1] Do your best to keep your present biases and hopes from influencing your decision. I commend you for joining me in this venture. May God's wisdom, discernment, perseverance, and guidance be given you in your quest.

Notes

Chapter 2 Paul's Opening Statement

1. Philippians 3:5–6.
2. Galatians 1:14.
3. Acts 9:4–6.
4. 1 Corinthians 15:17.
5. Josephus, *Jewish War* 6.304. See also 2.612; *Jewish Antiquities* 12.256. The writings of Josephus shed much light on life in the first century. For those interested in the best of Josephus in a fresh translation, the following is recommended: Paul L. Maier, *Josephus: The Essential Works* (Grand Rapids: Kregel, 1995).
6. *Martyrdom of Polycarp* 2.2.
7. Seneca, *Dialogue 7 (De vita beata)*, 19.3. Seneca, *Ad Lucilium Epistulae Morales*, trans. Richard M. Gummere, Loeb Classical Library, (Cambridge, MA: Harvard University Press, 1971), 3:164–67.
8. Josephus, *The Life* 420–21.
9. A number of these are mentioned in Raymond Brown, *The Death of the Messiah* (New York: Doubleday, 1994), 2:1088–92.
10. Cicero, *Orations*, Speech 13, 12.27; *Gospel of Peter* 4.14. The *Gospel of Peter* mentions an instance when breaking the legs was forbidden so that the crucified victim would suffer longer.
11. John Dominic Crossan, *Jesus: A Revolutionary Biography* (San Francisco: HarperCollins, 1994), 145.
12. Justin Martyr, *Trypho* 108; Tertullian, *De spectaculis* 30.
13. Paul L. Maier, *In the Fullness of Time: A Historian Looks at Christmas, Easter, and the Early Church* (Grand Rapids: Kregel, 1997), 198.

14. This concept of "resurrection" continued until the second-century Gnostics introduced a different meaning relating only to the raising of the spirit without a body. However, this does not threaten the argument here attributed to Paul, since it is within the first-century Jewish setting that talk of Jesus's resurrection appears.

15. Mark 12:26–27; Matthew 22:32; Luke 20:37–38.

16. William Wand, *Christianity: A Historical Religion?* (Valley Forge, PA: Judson, 1972), 93–94.

17. 1 Corinthians 15:3–8.

18. Atheist New Testament scholar Gerd Lüdemann says that the appearance traditions in the creed are "doubtless very old, since they all go back to the time before the appearance of Christ to Paul." See Gerd Lüdemann, *The Resurrection of Christ* (Amherst, NY: Prometheus, 2004), 31. Gerd Theissen and Annette Merz write, "the whole tradition in 15.3–7 will go back in substance to the time *before the Apostolic Council*. . . . It follows from this that there was already a stereotyped tradition about the death and resurrection of Jesus fifteen years after his death." See Gerd Theissen and Annette Merz, *The Historical Jesus* (Minneapolis: Fortress, 1996), 488. James D. G. Dunn writes, "This tradition, we can be entirely confident, was *formulated as tradition within months of Jesus's death.*" See James D. G. Dunn, *Jesus Remembered* (Grand Rapids: Eerdmans, 2003), 855.

19. 1 Corinthians 15:11.

20. 1 Corinthians 15:11–12, 14.

21. *1 Clement* 42:3: "Therefore, having received orders and complete certainty caused by the resurrection of our Lord Jesus Christ and believing in the Word of God, they went with the Holy Spirit's certainty, preaching the good news that the kingdom of God is about to come" (author's translation). Irenaeus reported that Clement had known the apostles. See Irenaeus, *Against Heresies*, Book 3, Chapter 3, Section 3, ca. AD 185 in A. Roberts, J. Donaldson, and A. C. Coxe, *The Ante-Nicene Fathers: Translations of the Writings of the Fathers Down to A.D. 325* (Oak Harbor, WA: Logos Research Systems, 1997). A few years later Tertullian reported that Peter had ordained Clement. See Tertullian, *The Prescription Against Heretics*, chapter 32, in Roberts, Donaldson, and Coxe.

22. Luke, Clement of Rome, Polycarp, Ignatius, Dionysius, Tertullian, Origen. For details see Gary R. Habermas and Michael R. Licona, *The Case for the Resurrection of Jesus* (Grand Rapids: Kregel, 2004), 56–62.

23. 1 Corinthians 15:9–10; Galatians 1:12–16, 22–23; Philippians 3:6–7.

24. Acts 7:58; 8:1–3; 9:1–19; 22:3–16; 26:9–23. For more on this, see Habermas and Licona, *The Case for the Resurrection of Jesus*, 64–66.

25. Galatians 1:23.

26. Paul (2 Cor. 11:23–28; Phil. 1:21–23), Luke (Acts 14:19; 16:19–24; 17:5; 17:13–15; 18:12–13; 21:27–36; 23:12–35), Clement (*1 Clem.* 5.2–7), Polycarp (*To the Philippians* 9.2), Tertullian (*Scorpiace* 15; also cited by Eusebius in *Ecclesiastical History* [*Hist. eccl.*] 2.25.8), Dionysius (cited by Eusebius in *Hist. eccl.* 2.25.8), Origen (*Commentary on Genesis* cited by Eusebius in *Hist. eccl.* 3.1).

27. Mark 6:3–4; John 7:5.

28. Acts 15:12–21; Galatians 1:19. Acts 1:14 and 1 Corinthians 9:5 indicate that more than one of Jesus's brothers became believers. Church tradition reports that two letters in the New Testament were authored by the brothers after whom they were named: James and Jude.

29. Josephus, *Jewish Antiquities* 20.200. The writings of Hegesippus and portions of Clement's writings are no longer extant. We are fortunate that fragments have been preserved in the writings of others. See Eusebius, *Hist. eccl.* 2.23.

30. We can only speculate when the appearance to James occurred. Luke reports that Jesus's brothers were gathered with his disciples and mother for constant prayer a few days before Pentecost (Acts 1:14), indicating that James had become a believer by then. This would place the appearance within fifty days of Jesus's resurrection.

31. Paula Fredriksen, *Jesus of Nazareth* (New York: Vintage, 1999), 264.

Chapter 3 Muhammad's Opening Statement

1. A sura is similar to a chapter. Each sura presents a complete thought and has no relation to those that precede and follow it.

2. Qur'an 2:23; cf. 10:37–38 and 17:88. *The Meaning of The Holy Qur'an*, New Edition with Revised Translation, Commentary and Newly Compiled Comprehensive Index, 10th edition, trans. Abdullah Yusuf Ali (Beltsville, MD: Amana, 1999). All quotations from the Qur'an cited henceforth are from this edition.

3. Qur'an, 4:157–58.

4. *Gospel of Barnabas* 215–20.

5. John 19:34.

6. Mark 15:44.

7. Matthew 27:15–24; Mark 15:6–14; Luke 23:4–6, 13–16, 20–22; John 18:38–39; 19:4–6, 12, 15.

8. Mark 15:39.

9. John Dominic Crossan, *The Historical Jesus: The Life of a Mediterranean Jewish Peasant* (San Francisco: HarperSanFrancisco, 1991), 392–93.

10. Raymond E. Brown, *The Virginal Conception and Bodily Resurrection of Jesus* (London: Geoffrey Chapman, 1974). Brown claims that many times in the Old Testament, the "angel of the Lord" is simply a way of describing God's speaking with men. He provides the example of Exodus 3:2 and notes that it says the angel of the Lord appeared in the bush, and just two verses later it is God who speaks through the bush (122).

11. Romans 1:3–4, 9; 5:10; 8:3, 29, 32; 1 Corinthians 1:9; 15:28; 2 Corinthians 1:19; Galatians 1:16; 2:20; 4:4, 6; Ephesians 4:13; Colossians 1:13; 2:9 (where all the fullness of deity is said presently to be in Jesus's body); 1 Thessalonians 1:10.

12. Qur'an 5:116. See also 5:72.

13. Qur'an 4:171. Also see 18:4–5.

Chapter 4 Paul's Rebuttal

1. Irrespective of what position one is arguing, the "bias objection" has a number of problems. First, as it pertains to Jesus's resurrection, Paul's testimony is stronger than that of a neutral witness of the risen Jesus, since Paul's bias ran in the *opposite* direction. He was certainly not sympathetic to the Christian cause. Rather, he viewed Jesus as a false Messiah and severely persecuted his followers. Second, James is another witness whose biases ran contrary to Christianity until he experienced the risen Jesus. Third, recognizing the bias of an author does not automatically merit the conclusion that he has distorted the facts. Modern-day Jewish historians of the Nazi holocaust have very carefully chronicled Nazi atrocities because they are passionately committed to exposing what really occurred, whereas revisionist historians most of whom are Gentile tend to downplay them. In this case, the bias of the person works in favor of historical accuracy. This third point is a summary of what Craig Blomberg said in the videotape series produced by David Cerullo and John Ankerberg, *Jesus: The Search Continues.* Two Tapes (Chattanooga, TN: Ankerberg Theological Research Institute, 2001), Tape 1. The role of the historian is to comb through the literature and attempt to see past the writer's personal biases in order to ascertain what really happened.

2. Mormons claim that the Book of Mormon is an account of a group of Jews who came to North or Central America around 600 BC. These grew to a large population that spoke and wrote in Hebrew and Egyptian. However, nothing has ever been found in North or Central America indicating that the inhabitants knew these languages. To complicate matters further, no artifacts have turned up where they certainly should be. For example, the Book of Mormon reports a large-scale battle at the hill Cumorah near Rochester, New York, where hundreds of thousands were killed and left unburied around the year AD 400. Archaeologists would expect many artifacts consistent with the account to be available if this account is true. These would include an abundance of skeletal remains and weapons. However, nothing has ever been found at the hill Cumorah that indicates a large-scale battle took place at the site. For more on this, see Michael R. Licona, *Behold, I Stand at the Door and Knock* (Virginia Beach: TruthQuest Publishers, 1998), chapters 3–4. Although this book is out of print, an electronic version of the text is available at www.risenjesus.com.

3. Objective beauty is certainly evident in ocean sunsets, flowery fields, and majestic mountains, but in other instances, superior beauty is not always obvious across cultures.

4. Mark 8:31 (Matthew 16:21; Luke 5:35); Mark 9:31 (Matthew 17:22–23; Luke 9:44); Mark 10:33–34 (Matthew 20:18–19; Luke 18:31–33); Mark 12:7–8 (Matthew 21:38–39; Luke 20:14–15); Mark 14:8 (Matthew 26:12).

5. See Robert W. Funk, Roy W. Hoover, and The Jesus Seminar, *The Five Gospels: What Did Jesus Really Say?* (San Francisco: HarperSanFrancisco, 1993), 100–101, 510–11. The Jesus Seminar holds that the *Gospel of Thomas* preserves the more authentic saying of Jesus. Even if they are correct, the same relevant points are made that we witness in Mark's version. Many schol-

ars are confident that Jesus uttered this parable for the following reasons: (1) Christian additions are absent where we would expect them. Nowhere is Jesus's vindication by God or resurrection mentioned, which we would expect the postresurrection church to include. (2) The parable perfectly suits Jesus's hostile and controversial situation. (3) It perfectly suits Palestinian life in the time of Jesus. Absentee landlords were common in Jesus's day. (4) Some scholars appeal to the historical inaccuracy related to the chronology of the death of Jesus. In Mark, he is first killed, then thrown out of the vineyard, whereas crucified victims were escorted outside the city walls, then crucified. Matthew and Luke write later than Mark and reverse the order to reflect the process more accurately. Many scholars hold that Mark reports the more accurate version and that Matthew and Luke corrected it. However, since it could be that Matthew and Luke got it right while Mark was inaccurate, the weight of an argument for authenticity given Mark's inaccurate order must be light. (5) A simpler version of the parable is found in the *Gospel of Thomas* (65), and thus we have multiple sources reporting the parable.

    6. Hengel provides a list in Martin Hengel, *Crucifixion* (Philadelphia: Fortress, 1977), 31–32nn25–26. The list includes: Philo, *De posteritate Caini* 61; *De somniis* 2.213; Achilles Tatius, *Leucippe et Clitophon* 2.37.3; Plutarch, *Moralia* 499D; Pliny the Elder, *Naturalis historia* 28.41–46; Ps. Manetho, *Apotelesmatica* 4.199; 1.149; Seneca, *Dialogue 7 (De vita beata)* 19.3; Lukan, *De Bello Civili* 6.543–47; Apuleius, *Metamorphoses* 3.17.4; Galen, *De usu partium* 12.11; Artemidorus, *Onirocritica* 2.56; Lucian, *Prometheus* 1.2; *Dialogus deorum* 5(1).1; and Xenophon of Ephesus, *Ephesiaca* 4.23, which mentions binding to the cross as an Egyptian practice. We may add that Josephus mentions nailing to the cross (*Jewish War* 4.451). Tacitus does not mention nails but reports how Nero fastened Christians to crosses and then in the evening set them ablaze to provide light for his gardens. It is difficult to imagine ropes being used here, since fire would burn through them (*Annals* 15.44).

    7. Yehohanan, the son of Hagakol. Yehohanan is estimated to have been a healthy young man in his mid to late twenties. He was approximately five feet six inches tall, lean, and had a cleft right palate. See Vassilios Tzaferis, "Crucifixion—The Archaeological Evidence," *Biblical Archaeology Review* 11 (January/February 1985): 1, Libronix Software (Oak Harbor, WA: Logos Research Systems, 1997).

    8. John 20:25. Luke alludes to nails in a resurrection appearance when Jesus says, "Look at my hands and my feet" (Luke 24:39).

    9. Cicero, *Orations*, Speech 13, 12.27 and *Gospel of Peter* 4:14. This is precisely the reason John reports that the legs of the thieves were broken—because it was the eve of the Passover. The Talmud *Sanhedrian* 43a also reports that Jesus was crucified on the eve of the Passover.

    10. Josephus, *Jewish War* 4.317.

    11. The archaeological find of Yehohanan mentioned in note 7 above is certainly consistent with this. The remains were in an ossuary or bone box, proof in stone that the victim had received a proper burial rather than been discarded in a common pit as Crossan suggests ("Crucifixion—The Archaeological Evidence," *Biblical Archaeological Review*). It should also be

noted that Crossan has since softened his view and allows the possibility that Jesus was buried. During a meeting of the Evangelical Theological Society in San Antonio, Texas, on November 19, 2004, after Crossan had read a paper titled *A Response to N. T. Wright's Response to His Critics*, he told me that he would not be at all surprised to learn that there was an empty tomb where Jesus had been laid and that Paul believed in an empty tomb.

12. John 19:31.

13. Quintilian, *Declamationes maiores* 6.9, http://www.gmu.edu/depart ments/fld/CLASSICS/quintilian.decl.mai6.html.

14. Special thanks to Dr. Jim Ritchie, Emergency Medicine Residency Director of Portsmouth Naval Hospital in Portsmouth, Virginia, for providing this and related insights.

15. John 19:23–24, 28, 31–37. Also see 13:18; 17:12 where John sees theological significance in the betrayal by Judas.

16. I would like to thank my friend Mary Beth Watson for this example.

17. E. P. Sanders's book *Paul and Palestinian Judaism* (Minneapolis: Augsburg Fortress, 1977) is regarded to have sounded the death knell to the view that Paul invented Christianity.

Chapter 5 Muhammad's Rebuttal

1. Qur'an 4:171.

2. Genesis 20:2, 7.

3. See Maurice Bucaille, *The Bible, The Qur'an and Science*, 6th rev. ed. (Chicago: Kazi, 1977), available online at http://www.tempemasjid.com/mau rice/frcont15.htm. See also I. A. Ibrahim, ed., *A Brief Illustrated Guide to Understanding Islam*, 2nd ed. (Houston: Darussalam, 1997), 5–31. However, an article posted on IslamOnline.net on March 23, 2004, titled "Scientific Research in Qur'an Should Be Based on Sound Methods: Conference," discussed how a Muslim organization named The International Commission on the Scientific Miraculous Nature in the Qur'an and Sunnah convened to discuss the relationship between science and the Qur'an. Fifteen non-Muslim scientists from Japan, the United States, France, and Germany were asked to attend the conference and then provide their opinions on the strength of the evidence presented. One scientist commented that while the presentations were interesting, many contained misinformation, and much was not based on fact. Another scientist said she saw no relation between the scientific evidence produced and the Qur'an. The article reported no affirming comments from any of the scientists. See http://www.islamonline.net/English/In_Depth/ Scientific_Reflections/2004/03/article02.shtml. For a detailed answer to the claim that science affirms the Qur'an, see William Campbell, *The Qur'an and the Bible in the Light of History and Science*, 2nd ed. (Upper Darby, PA: Middle East Resources, 2002), available online at http://answering-islam.org .uk/Campbell/contents.html.

4. See *Psalms of Solomon* 16:4 and 3 Maccabees 5:14.

5. Romans 12:5; 1 Corinthians 10:16–17; 12:12–27 (esp. v. 27); Ephesians 1:22–23; 3:6; 4:4, 12, 16; 5:23, 30; Colossians 1:18, 24; 2:19; 3:15.

6. 1 Corinthians 15:44.

7. 1 Corinthians 15:44 NRSV.

8. Acts 2 states that it was on the day of Pentecost that the disciples started preaching that Jesus had risen from the dead. Pentecost was a Jewish holiday that celebrated Moses receiving the Law on Mt. Sinai fifty days after leaving Egypt, or fifty days after the day after the Passover.

Chapter 6 Discussion Period: Part One

1. Irenaeus, *Against Heresies* 3.3.3 (ca. AD 185) and Tertullian, *Prescription against Heretics* 32 (ca. AD 200). For more information on Clement and Polycarp, see Habermas and Licona, *The Case for the Resurrection of Jesus*, 53–55.

2. *1 Clement* (ca. AD 95) and Polycarp, *To the Philippians* (ca. AD 110).

3. *1 Clement* 5:1–5 (author's translation).

4. Pol. *Phil.* 3:2 (author's translation).

5. See, for example, Justin Martyr, *First Apology* (66): "For the apostles, in the memoirs composed by them, which are called Gospels, have thus delivered unto us what was enjoined upon them; that Jesus took bread, and when He had given thanks, said, 'This do in remembrance of Me, this is My body'; and that, after the same manner, having taken the cup and given thanks, He said, 'This is My blood'; and gave it to them alone." A. Roberts, J. Donaldson, and A. C. Coxe, *The Ante-Nicene Fathers, vol. 1* (Oak Harbor, WA: Logos Research Systems, 1997). Justin refers to the Gospels as the "memoirs" of the apostles and then quotes from them. In his *Dialogue with Trypho*, Justin makes mention of these "memoirs" another thirteen times (100–107). In every instance he either quotes from a Gospel or relates a story from them.

6. Craig L. Blomberg, *The Historical Reliability of John's Gospel* (Downers Grove, IL: InterVarsity, 2001), 22–41; F. F. Bruce, *The Gospel and Epistles of John* (Grand Rapids: Eerdmans, 1983), 1–12; John Drane, *Introducing the New Testament* (Minneapolis: Fortress, 2001), 197, 200–201, where he states confidence in the traditional authorship of Mark and Luke; R. T. France, *The Gospel of Mark*, The New International Greek Testament Commentary (Grand Rapids: Eerdmans, 2002), 35–41; R. T. France, *Matthew: Evangelist and Teacher* (Downers Grove, IL: InterVarsity, 1989), 50–80; Donald Guthrie, *New Testament Introduction*, rev. ed. (Downers Grove, IL: InterVarsity, 1990), 43–53, 81–84, 113–25, 252–83; Craig S. Keener, *The Gospel of John, A Commentary*, vol. 1 (Peabody, MA: Hendrickson, 2003), 82–104.

7. AD 51.

8. 1 Corinthians 15:3–5.

9. For example, "sins," whereas Paul uses "sin" elsewhere; "according to the Scriptures," whereas Paul usually uses "it is written" elsewhere; "he was seen" (also can be translated "he appeared") is absent elsewhere in Paul's letters; "the Twelve" is found only in this creed in Paul's letters. See Theissen and Merz, *The Historical Jesus*, 487.

10. Acts 15.

11. Galatians 2:1–10.

Notes

12. Eusebius, *Evangelical Preparation for the Gospel*, 12.31: *hoti deēsei pote tō psudei anti pharmakou chrēsthai ep ōpheleia tōn deomenōn tou toioutou tropou* (When it will be necessary to lie as a remedy to make use of for the benefit of those who like this way).
13. Plato, *Laws* 663D.
14. The Greek is *agatho pseudesthai*.
15. R. G. Bury, *Plato in Twelve Volumes*, Loeb Classical Library Series (Cambridge: Harvard University Press, 1914–1935), 10:125.
16. Specifically, anthropopatheia (anthropopathism).
17. Psalm 120:2; Proverbs 6:16–19; 12:19, 22; Romans 3:7–8; Colossians 3:9; 1 John 2:21; Revelation 21:27; 22:15.

Chapter 7 Discussion Period: Part Two

1. See Ibn Ishaq, *Sirat Rasul Allah*, trans. Alfred Guillaume (Oxford: Ameena Saiyid, 2004), 71–73, 106. This work is known as *The Life of Muhammad* and is the oldest biography of Muhammad.
2. Matthew 12:40.
3. James D. G. Dunn, *Jesus Remembered*, 823: "The earliest versions of the tradition attributed to Jesus envisage being raised 'after three days.' The phrase almost certainly means 'soon,' 'shortly' (in a short time), as in the equivalent time interval envisaged in Luke 13:32–33."
4. Esther 4:16 NASB. The Greek is *epi hēmeras treis nukta kai hēmeran* (for three days, night and day).
5. The Greek is *en tē hēmera tē tritē*.
6. Esther 5:1 NASB.
7. Matthew 16:21 (*tē tritē hēmera*); 17:23 (*tē tritē hēmera*); 20:19 (*tē tritē hēmera*); cf. 26:61 (*dia triōn hēmerōn*).
8. Mark 8:31; 9:31; 10:33–34; 12:7–8; 14:8.
9. See chapter 4, note 5 above.

Chapter 8 Discussion Period: Part Three

1. A potentially fatal state due to a decrease in volume of circulating blood.
2. John 10:17–18. Cf. Matthew 26:53–54: At his arrest in Gethsemane, Jesus tells Peter to put away his sword. "Do you think I cannot call on my Father, and he will at once put at my disposal more than twelve legions of angels? But how then would the Scriptures be fulfilled that say it must happen in this way?" (probably referring to Zech. 13:7).
3. John 19:12.
4. Mark 15:39.
5. Mark 15:33.
6. Matthew 27:51–53.
7. A number of sources later reported that these were real persons who were raised by Jesus. Ignatius speaks of the prophets raised by Jesus (*To the Magnesians* 9.2). Quadratus (117–138) reported that they existed a considerable time and some even still lived (*Ecclesiastical History* 4.3.2). *Acts of Pilate*

17.1 says Jesus raised Simeon and his two sons, that their tombs could still be seen opened, that they were alive and dwelling in Arimathea, and that people had gone and talked with them. In addition, the darkness is multiply-attested by the Synoptics and the secular historian Thallus (AD 52). The rending of the veil is multiply-attested by the Synoptics. Finally, destructive earthquakes were common in the region and can explain four of the six phenomena. See Tacitus, *Annals*, 2.47; 4.13, 55; 12.43, 58; 14.27; 15.22; Suetonius, *Twelve Caesars*: Augustus 47; Tiberius 8, 48, 74; Caligula 37; Claudius 22; Nero 20, 48; Galba 18; Vespasian 17; Josephus, *Jewish Antiquities* 15.121–22, 142; *Jewish War* 1.370–73, 377–78; 380–81; 4.285–87.

8. "On Providence," Fragment 2, section 50, in Eusebius's *Evangelical Preparation of the Gospel*.

9. Plutarch, *Caesar* 69.4.

10. Ovid, *Fasti* 2.493.

11. Cicero, *De republica* 6.22.

12. Virgil, *Georgica*, Georgic 1.466–97. In this fascinating passage, Virgil reports that when Caesar died there was darkness, dogs and birds acted strangely, Etna erupted, fighting in the heavens was heard, the Alps were shaken, a powerful voice was heard, pale phantoms were seen at dusk, cattle spoke, streams stood still, ivory idols wept, bronze idols sweat, lightning in cloudless skies, a comet, and a few other signs. Virgil reports many more details than do others just as Matthew provides more than the other Gospel writers. While these details are of interest, it should be noted that Virgil here writes in certain poetic language that we would not expect to understand as history. Matthew does not write in the same genre. However, this does not necessarily rule out his minor use of this genre in his additional details.

13. Josephus, *Ant.* 14.309.

14. See Joel 2:10, where similar language is certain to be metaphorical.

15. Cassius Dio, *History* 51.17:5: *kai nekrōn eidōla ephantadzeto*; author's translation.

16. John 19:34.

17. Maier, *In the Fullness of Time*, 180. The fire itself is unquestioned and is a minimal fact. This is what historians refer to as a "basic layer of historical truth." Historians believe they can identify this basic layer in the worst of thirdhand sources. See A. N. Sherwin-White, *Roman Society and Roman Law in the New Testament* (New York: Oxford, 1963), 186.

18. See chapter 5, note 3.

19. Although Habermas has yet to publish all the results, he has touched on some of the more important ones in Gary R. Habermas, *The Risen Jesus and Future Hope* (New York: Rowman and Littlefield, 2003), chapter 1, and Habermas and Licona, *The Case for the Resurrection of Jesus*, chapters 3 and 4.

Chapter 9 Discussion Period: Part Four

1. Josephus, *Jewish War* 3.335.

Notes

2. "As for those who die on the cross, the executioner does not forbid the burying of those who have been pierced" (Quintilian, *Declamationes maiores* 6.9). The Latin term is *percussos*, which means "to strike through and through, thrust through, pierce, transfix" (Gregory R. Crane, ed., "Perseus Word Study Tool," The Perseus Project, http://www.perseus.tufts.edu).

3. See H. G. Liddell, R. Scott, H. S. Jones, and R. McKenzie, *A Greek-English Lexicon*, Ninth Edition with Revised Supplement (New York: Oxford, 1996), 1983. Many believe Jesus was nailed in the wrists, which could easily be considered part of the hand.

4. "The probability that death was the result of asphyxiation appears likely because of what is known of certain German practices. A 1937 book by Dr. Hynek of Prague describes a military punishment, the 'aufbinden,' which he witnessed when serving in the German army in 1914–18. The punished soldier was hanged by the hands on a post, the tips of his toes barely reaching the ground. After a while, the muscles of the arms, thorax, and legs began to contract violently. Because the thorax muscles commanding inhaling are stronger than those commanding exhaling the lungs filled to the maximum, but they could not expel the air turned into carbon dioxide. To avoid death by asphyxiation, the tortured soldier was let down for a short time and then lifted up again. The Nazis used this method for torture and execution in their deportation camps according to former Dachau prisoners." John Rousseau and Rami Arav, *Jesus and His World* (Minneapolis: Fortress, 1995), 75. Two known experiments simulating crucifixion using volunteers have been published. Medical examiner Fred Zugibe positioned the arms of the volunteers at 60 to 70 degree angles. In this position, asphyxiation was not a problem. However, Zugibe cites another study done by radiologist Hermann Moedder, who had a number of volunteers suspended from two-by-fours with their arms positioned about 41 inches apart and angled between 45 to 30 degrees. The victims would lose consciousness in no more than twelve minutes. For Zugibe's findings, see Frederick T. Zugibe, *The Cross and the Shroud: A Medical Examiner Investigates the Crucifixion* (Cresskill, NJ: McDonagh and Company, 1981), 68–70, 94–95, 105. Moedder's findings are reported in Robert K. Wilcox, *Shroud* (New York: Macmillan, 1977), 23–25, 161.

5. See Moedder's findings in the previous note.

6. See Zugibe's findings in note 4 above.

7. "If both legs were broken at or below the knees, there are no medical reasons why this would expedite death other than preventing ventilation. If both legs were broken above the knees (i.e., at the femurs), death became a very significant possibility, since it could, but not necessarily would, cause a large amount of blood to fill the legs. In this case the victim would bleed to death. This would not be immediate but could take as little as just under an hour" (James V. Ritchie, M.D., Emergency Medicine Residency Director, Portsmouth Naval Hospital, Portsmouth, Virginia, in personal conversation with the author). It is interesting to note here that the skeletal remains of a crucified victim were discovered in Jerusalem in 1968. One of his shins had been shattered and the other fractured (see chapter 4, note 7).

Notes

8. The *Gospel of Barnabas* (215–20) makes the claim that when Judas and the crowd came for Jesus, four angels took Jesus up to heaven and God made Judas look and sound like Jesus so that everyone was convinced. Judas was crucified and buried in Joseph's tomb. Then some of the less spiritual disciples of Jesus came at night, stole the body of Judas (thinking it was the body of Jesus), hid it, and proclaimed he had risen. Then Jesus made request of Allah that he would let him visit his grieving mother. His request was granted, and he appeared to his mother as well as Martha, Mary, Lazarus, Barnabas, John, James, and Peter. Then the four angels who accompanied him explained what God had done in saving Jesus.

9. There is no evidence that the *Gospel of Barnabas* existed prior to the fifteenth century. No manuscripts of it are older than the fifteenth century. No one cites it prior to the fifteenth century. It is never mentioned by the early church fathers or by Muslim apologists who were engaged in constant debates with Christians throughout the first eight centuries of Islam's existence (i.e., the seventh through fourteenth centuries). The only early mention of a *Gospel of Barnabas* is in a fifth-century document called The Gelasian Decree written by Pope Gelasius in AD 492–495. The only mention is its name and that it was a spurious book rejected by the church. However, since the *Gospel of Barnabas* contains medieval anachronisms, this reference is probably referring to a different *Gospel of Barnabas*. These anachronisms suggest a date in the Middle Ages. For example, the Year of Jubilee is said to occur every one hundred years (chapter 83). However, the Year of Jubilee was celebrated every fifty years until a papal decree in AD 1343, placing the date of writing sometime afterward. Medieval feudalism is mentioned in chapter 122 and medieval court procedures in chapter 121. Someone in the first century would not have known about these things. Wooden wine casks are mentioned in chapter 152 instead of the wineskins which were used in first-century Palestine. The *Gospel of Barnabas* also contains a striking contradiction that would rule out Barnabas as its true author. The Hebrew/Aramaic word "Messiah" was translated "Christ" in Greek by first-century Christians. The *Gospel of Barnabas* makes the mistake of referring to Jesus as "Christ" on at least two occasions in the first two sentences of the Gospel only to later deny that he is the Messiah (chapters 42, 70, 82, 96, 97, 198, 206). This is a mistake that Barnabas would certainly not have made, since he would have been well acquainted with both Hebrew/Aramaic and Greek. Moreover, the Qur'an affirms that Jesus is the Messiah (sura 3:45), thus contradicting the *Gospel of Barnabas*.

10. Around AD 185, Irenaeus quoted the Gnostic Valentinus as saying this around AD 140 (*Against Heresies* 1:24:4).

11. Raymond E. Brown, *The Death of the Messiah* (New York: Doubleday, 1994), 2:1092–94.

12. Qur'an 3:49.

13. Qur'an 5:110.

14. "The Infancy Gospel of Thomas," in *Lost Scriptures: Books That Did Not Make It into the New Testament*, ed. Bart D. Ehrman (New York: Oxford University Press, 2003), 58.

15. Cf. Qur'an 5.29–34.
16. 1 Corinthians 15:11 (ca. AD 56–57).
17. Galatians 2:1–2, 7–9 (ca. AD 50–58).
18. Examples include Acts 2:22–32; 10:38–43; 13:26–41.

Chapter 10 Discussion Period: Part Five

1. I (the author) questioned a medical examiner. Unfortunately, I did not obtain a name.

2. Tacitus, *Annals*, Books 8–14, trans. John Jackson, Loeb Classical Library (Cambridge, MA: Harvard University Press, 1981), 5:283–85.

3. Tacitus's probable reference to Christianity as a "pernicious superstition" and also "evil" makes him a hostile source, adding weight to affirming details of his testimony with historians.

4. Galatians 1:18; 2:1–9.

5. Acts 15:1–29. The critical scholar Paula Fredriksen lists the disciples' permanent relocation to Jerusalem as "historical bedrock" and one of the facts known past doubting about the earliest community after Jesus's death. See Fredriksen, *Jesus of Nazareth*, 264.

6. For an exhaustive treatment on the subject, see N. T. Wright, *The Resurrection of the Son of God* (Minneapolis: Fortress, 2003).

7. Matthew 28:3; Mark 9:3; John 20:12; Acts 1:10; 10:30. See also Daniel 7:9.

8. In Tobit 5:5, 7, and 10, the angel is addressed as "young man"; Acts 1:10; 10:30; Luke 24:4, 23.

9. Romans 12:5; 1 Corinthians 10:16–7; 12:12–27 (esp. 27); Ephesians 1:22–23; 3:6; 4:4, 12, 16; 5:23, 30; Colossians 1:18, 24; 2:19; 3:15.

10. Origen, *Contra Celsum* 2.55, 59. Greek text used is Origen, *Contra Celsum, Libri 8* (Leiden: Brill, 2001), 127, 131: *ek tēs autēs goēteias*. The translation "a conspiracy" is the author's.

11. 1 Corinthians 15:20.

12. Exceptions include the New English Bible, "animal," and the Amplified Bible, "natural (physical)."

13. This word is pronounced psu-ki-kos.

14. Paul uses it three other times, all in the same letter: 1 Corinthians 2:14; 15:44 (two times), 46. Also see James 3:15, which employs the term to contrast a proper spiritual state of the heart with one that is not from God and which is described as "earthly," "natural" (*psychikos*), and "demonic." Jude 1:19 uses the word to describe the lost who do not have the Holy Spirit and who live by "natural instinct" (*psychikos*). The only other appearances of the term in ancient Jewish literature are in 2 Maccabees 4:37 and 14:24, where it means "heartily" in reference to feelings of grief and warmth, and in 4 Maccabees 1:32, where it refers to a bodily appetite.

15. This word is pronounced nu-ma-ti-kos.

16. See 1 Corinthians 2:15; 3:1; 14:37 (cf. Galatians 6:1) where it refers to the spiritually mature in this world. See 1 Corinthians 2:13–14; 9:11; 10:3–4; 12:1; 14:1 where it refers to something that has to do with or has as its origin

in the Holy Spirit. Other occurrences in Paul's letters include Romans 1:11; 7:14; 15:27; Galatians 6:1; Ephesians 1:3; 5:19; 6:12; Colossians 1:9; 3:16. With the possible exception of Ephesians 6:12, which is unclear, Paul never used the term to describe something as "immaterial." Outside of Paul, the word only appears in 1 Peter 2:5 and Revelation 11:8. It does not appear in the LXX or the Jewish intertestamental books.

17. See Genesis 2:7 (LXX) where the Greek for "became a living soul" is identical, indicating that Paul appears to have this verse in mind when he writes 1 Corinthians 15:45.

18. Romans 8:11.

19. *zōopoieō.*

20. Words attributed to God in Psalm 95:7–11 are attributed to the Holy Spirit in Hebrews 3:7–11. The Holy Spirit is called God in Acts 5:3–5. God and Jesus are both referred to as the (a) Alpha and Omega (Revelation 21:6; 1:8; 22:13), (b) First and Last (Isaiah 44:6; Revelation 1:17–18; 22:13), (c) Beginning and End (Revelation 21:6; 1:17–18; 2:8; 22:13). God and Jesus are both said to have performed the creation in Genesis 1:1; John 1:3; Colossians 1:15. Paul cited Joel 3:5 which referred to God and applied it to Jesus in Romans 10:13. The author of Hebrews applied to Jesus a psalm addressed to God: Hebrews 1:8–9; cf. Psalm 45:7–8. The most satisfactory interpretation of Psalm 45:7–8 is that the psalmist addressed "God." Notwithstanding, the LXX and the author of Hebrews leave little doubt that this is how they meant it when translating and quoting the passage and applying it to Jesus. See Murray J. Harris, *Jesus as God* (Grand Rapids: Baker, 1992), 187–227. Raymond Brown agrees in *An Introduction to New Testament Christology* (New York: Paulist, 1994), 185–87.

21. *Shirk* means "associating partners with Allah. Shirk can also encompass any object that a person may hold in regard higher than Allah. It is the most severe of sins and will not be forgiven." Islamic Server of MSA-USC, *Glossary of Islamic Terms and Concepts*, http://www.usc.edu/dept/MSA/reference/glossary/term.SHIRK.html, s.v. "Shirk."

22. Qur'an 4:171.

23. Qur'an 5:116.

24. Romans 3:4.

Chapter 11 Discussion Period: Part Six

1. Matthew 28:17.

2. Matthew 28:9; cf. John 20:17.

3. For a few of these, see Habermas and Licona, *The Case for the Resurrection*, 159–60. An additional explanation not included in Habermas and Licona is that Matthew is expressing a figure of speech such as when we refer to the spectacular comeback of the Boston Red Sox to win the 2004 World Series as "unbelievable." In support of this interpretation is Luke's use of a term stronger than *doubt* when the disciples saw Jesus. Luke 24:41 reports, "And yet while [the disciples were] marveling and *unbelieving from their joy*, he said to them, 'Do you have anything here to eat?'" Luke seems

here to communicate that the disciples saw Jesus, they were thrilled by it, and it was as though it was too good to be true.

4. For example John 3:16; 1 Timothy 2:3–4; 1 John 2:2.

5. Acts 1:14; cf. Mark 3:21, 31; 6:3–4; John 7:5.

6. Acts 9; 22; 26.

7. Luke 24:16.

8. Luke 24:31.

9. See Stephen T. Davis, "Seeing the Risen Jesus" in Stephen T. Davis, Daniel Kendall, and Gerald O'Collins, eds., *The Resurrection* (New York: Oxford, 1998), 136.

10. Although in disagreement, R. T. France notes "the virtually unanimous verdict of modern textual scholarship, that the authentic text of Mark available to us ends at 16:8" (France, *The Gospel of Mark*, 685). For a contrary view, N. Clayton Croy argues that both the beginning and ending of Mark have been lost. See N. Clayton Croy, *The Mutilation of Mark's Gospel* (Nashville: Abingdon, 2003).

11. See Dunn, *Jesus Remembered*, 833n26.

12. Tertullian, *Prescription against Heretics*, chap. 32.

13. Acts 9; 22; 26.

14. See Crossan, *Jesus: A Revolutionary Biography*, 169.

15. Acts 13:36–37.

16. Romans 8:11; 1 Corinthians 15:53; Philippians 3:21; 1 Thessalonians 5:23. This last reference is important since Paul elsewhere equates our mode of resurrection with that of Jesus (see Rom. 8:11; 1 Cor. 15:20; Phil. 3:21).

17. Four formulas: 1 Corinthians 15:3; Romans 1:3–4; 10:9; Philippians 2:8. Seventeen passages where Paul said "resurrection" or "raised from dead": Acts 17:18, 31–32; 26:23; Romans 4:24; 6:4–5, 9; 7:4; 8:11; 1 Corinthians 15:12–20; Galatians 1:1; Philippians 3:10; Colossians 2:12; 1 Thessalonians 1:10; cf. Ephesians 1:20; Acts 13:30, 34. Thirteen passages where Paul said "Christ died": Romans 5:6, 8, 10; 8:34; 14:9, 15; 1 Corinthians 8:11; 2 Corinthians 15:14–15; Galatians 2:21; Colossians 2:20; 1 Thessalonians 4:14; 5:10.

18. *Apocalypse of Peter* 81:4–24.

Chapter 12 Discussion Period: Part Seven

1. *The Stanford Encyclopedia of Philosophy*, Fall 2004 ed., s.v. "Charles Hartshorne," (by Dan Dombrowski) http://plato.stanford.edu/archives/fall2004/entries/hartshorne/.

2. Terry L. Miethe, ed., *Did Jesus Rise from the Dead?* (San Francisco: Harper and Row, 1987), 142.

3. See Sarah Coakley, "Response" in Davis, Kendall, O'Collins, *The Resurrection*, 184. Sarah Coakley is distinguished professor of divinity at Harvard.

4. In a survey of French, German, and English sources that touch on the subject of the resurrection of Jesus written between 1975–2005, Habermas discovered that of those scholars making a pronouncement of historical, nonhistorical, or unknown, approximately 75 percent awarded historicity,

concluding that Jesus rose from the dead in either a bodily or nonbodily sense. Habermas further discovered that approximately 75 percent of those awarding historicity also held that Jesus rose bodily. This is a huge change from the scholarly consensus of the two decades prior to 1975. See Gary R. Habermas, "Mapping the Recent Trend toward the Bodily Resurrection Appearances of Jesus in Light of Other Prominent Critical Positions," in Robert Stewart, ed., *The Resurrection of Jesus: John Dominic Crossan and N. T. Wright in Dialogue* (Minneapolis: Fortress, 2006 forthcoming).

Chapter 13 Muhammad's Closing Statement

1. Qur'an 29:2–5.
2. Romans 3:4 NLT. The citation is from Psalm 51:4 in the ancient Greek translation of the Old Testament called the Septuagint.

Chapter 14 Paul's Closing Statement

1. Wright, *The Resurrection of the Son of God*, 706.
2. Ibid., 19.
3. That it would be soon is indicated in Mark 10:33–34 (see also Matthew 20:18–19; Luke 18:31–33).
4. Proverbs 26:27.
5. Romans 8:16.
6. Acts 13:38–41, citing Habakkuk 1:5.
7. Philippians 3:4–11.
8. Matthew 10:37–39.

Chapter 15 Moderator's Conclusion

1. The interested reader may wish to go back and reread all of the arguments, making an outline of them. Then make notes next to each argument concerning how Paul or Muhammad answered it or whether he did. Then determine whether you find his answer convincing.

Michael R. Licona (Ph.D. cand., University of Pretoria) is director of apologetics evangelism at the North American Mission Board of the Southern Baptist Convention. He frequently speaks to churches, parachurch groups, and university audiences across the country. He is also the co-author of the award-winning *The Case for the Resurrection of Jesus*.